# RENEGADE MILLIONAIRE

DAN S. KENNEDY
WITH LEE MILTEER
FOREWORD BY ADAM WITTY

# RENEGADE MILLIONAIRE

## 7 SECRETS to Extreme Wealth, Autonomy, and Entrepreneurial Success

Advantage®

Published by Advantage, Charleston, South Carolina.
Member of Advantage Media Group.

ADVANTAGE is a registered trademark, and the Advantage colophon is a trademark of Advantage Media Group, Inc.

Printed in the United States of America.

10 9 8 7 6 5 4 3 2 1

ISBN: 978-1-64225-182-1
LCCN: 2020934960

Edited by Jack Turk.
Cover design by Carly Blake.
Layout design by Megan Elger.

CONTENTS

# FOREWORD

## BY ADAM WITTY

I'm Adam Witty, CEO of ***Dan Kennedy's Magnetic Marketing.*** I remember the first time I heard about Dan Kennedy.

It was August of 2006 and I had signed up for the MOST INCREDIBLE FREE GIFT EVER … and for only $19.97, I got to test drive three free months of membership to Dan Kennedy's ***NO B.S. Magnetic Marketing Letter***.

I was only a year into my business, and at that

time, my business was small. It was just me and one other person. We were working out of the spare bedroom in my home; my desk was actually *in* my bedroom. At the time, I was struggling just to stay afloat and keep the doors to my business open. I remember it like yesterday.

I remember the newsletter arriving at my doorstep … walking into my office (bedroom), closing the door, and lying in bed … reading it from front cover to back page.

I remember it being referred to as "A Marketing Seminar in Print"—and it sure felt that way to me.

I remember for two and a half hours I underlined, I highlighted, I found so many great ideas.

The *NO B.S. Magnetic Marketing Letter* was literally my marketing plan for the next thirty days—I had at least three, four, or five marketing campaigns ready to put into action over the next month.

I also remember on the very back page of that issue of the *NO B.S. Magnetic Marketing Letter*, was a piece written by Dan labeled:

**"Dan Kennedy's Renegade Millionaire System"**

You see, in every issue since its founding, up until even today, the back page of the letter has always been focused on the idea of becoming a "Renegade Millionaire."

Now the first time I saw that label Renegade Millionaire, I thought, "Well, this really doesn't apply to me."

You see, I've never thought of myself as a Renegade. In fact, I've thought of myself more as a Boy Scout (I'm an Eagle Scout by the way), and when it comes to the manner in which I've conducted my life and my business … well, gee, I just don't think you would use the word ***RENEGADE*** to describe what I've done.

But as I read more and more of those back pages, I realized that being a Renegade Millionaire wasn't about acting like some Harley-riding, smoking, drinking, bushy-bearded, burly kind of guy.

A Renegade Millionaire was more about nurturing a contrary mindset, thinking different, and having a worldview that entrepreneurs can leverage to attract and create success.

In fact, for Dan Kennedy, being a Renegade entrepreneur meant going against the grain, defying industry norms, and putting yourself and your business into a category of one.

You see, when Dan Kennedy talked about Renegade Millionaires, he was talking about people like Herb Kelleher, the cofounder of Southwest Airlines, who challenged the conventional wisdom of the airline industry:

- He only flew ONE type of airplane, the Boeing 737.
- He had only ONE class of service with no assigned seats.
- He did not serve meals and he surely did not give you a blanket if you were cold.
- He didn't follow the hub and spoke model, instead he built a point-to-point route system so you could get places direct and non-stop.
- He focused on cutting the costs out of running an airline, so he could give those cost savings back to the passengers. "Low

Fares" became the mantra of Southwest.

Southwest's Herb Kelleher was the ultimate Renegade. He redefined industry norms. He ignored conventional wisdom. When competitors went left, Herb went right—creating a new model for his industry, resulting in one of the most valuable airlines in the world.

And so, after reading Herb's story and the stories of other Renegade Millionaires, I realized …

## I WANTED TO BE A RENEGADE MILLIONAIRE TOO!

Of course, when I started my business in 2005, I wanted to be a success, which at that time was defined by a business making $1 million or more … thereby producing a comfortable life for me and my family.

And the Renegade Millionaire principles I applied to build and grow this business have created freedom and autonomy and enjoyment for me that otherwise I never would have dreamed possible.

**BEING A RENEGADE MILLIONAIRE** has taken that first business I started in my bedroom and grown it to become Advantage|ForbesBooks—experts in Authority Marketing and one of the largest independent business book publishers in the country. It's now a large business, employing over 75 people throughout the United States and serving over 1,500 customers in 14 countries.

**BEING A RENEGADE MILLIONAIRE** has also given me the opportunity to do things that I really, really love. For example, my wife Erin and I love to travel around the world. That requires freedom. It requires autonomy. And it also requires a little bit of coin in your pocket. And I credit all that to Dan Kennedy's timeless Renegade Millionaire principles.

**BEING A RENEGADE MILLIONAIRE** enabled me, in 2018, to purchase GKIC, which is now ***Dan Kennedy's Magnetic Marketing***. We're working very hard to make this the place that entrepreneurs go for refuge in the lonely world that we all live in.

As I look back over the years since getting that first *NO B.S. Magnetic Marketing Letter*, where I first learned about becoming a Renegade Millionaire, I now realize that the principles you'll discover in this book have been the reason, the jet fuel, for the growth and success we've had.

My great hope is that you will take some of these Renegade Millionaire principles and habits and integrate them into your life and into your business, and you'll reap the results as I and so many other Renegade Millionaires have.

And when you finish this book, if you're truly an exceptional entrepreneur, we hope that you might consider joining us and being a part of our Renegade Millionaire Mastermind where we are growing each other and our businesses and taking them to the next level.

**BEING A RENEGADE MILLIONAIRE** is a challenge, a journey, and an adventure like no other.

I trust that you, like me many years ago, can't wait to get started!

# PREFACE

This book is based on multiple interviews, presentations, and writings from Dan Kennedy, Lee Milteer, and Adam Witty on precisely what it takes and what it means to live out your entrepreneurial journey as a RENEGADE MILLIONAIRE.

Dan, Lee, and Adam each provided their own unique perspective and experience—both as individuals exploring this path and as leaders helping others along the way.

Rather than call out specifically who said what where when, you'll find it's written as if coming from a single voice ... because their passion and their mindset when it comes to living out the RENEGADE MILLIONAIRE lifestyle is practically identical.

In case you were wondering, this book is NOT about tactics—you know, mechanical details, one kind of mailing versus another, top ten fear factors to supersize your offers, that kind of thing.

Sure, some tactics work their way into the text ... but that's not what this is all about—this is a very frank, candid discussion about the very core of the ways that we—and other RENEGADE

MILLIONAIRES—fundamentally, creatively, and determinedly GO AGAINST THE FLOW and RUN INTO THE FIRE.

You'll discover how to recognize and break free of your "instinctive survival behaviors"—which run counter to profitable creativity and real innovation. You'll profit from new ways to analyze your market, your competition, the way things are being sold to your customers—the "behind the scenes" inside dish on how RENEGADE MILLIONAIRE Marketers tackle a target audience differently.

You'll learn how to defy conventional business metrics and instead "Flip The Equation"—this is the real NEW MATH and it's the most profound difference between the way RENEGADE MILLIONAIRES think of our businesses and the way 95 percent of business owners think about theirs.

In this book you're going to discover big and important ideas, vital principles, major strategies—and the 7 Key Secrets to you becoming a RENEGADE MILLIONAIRE as well.

Let's roll.

# INTRODUCTION

RENEGADE MILLIONAIRE—a lot of people have a serious block when it comes to the term "Renegade" and thinking of themselves in that way.

I think this goes back to the programming we received from our childhood, in the sense that all of us are programmed by the time we're seven years old by our society, our parents, the church we go to, just the environments we were in.

And if you were called a "Renegade," it was almost a pox upon you—because you weren't following the rules, you weren't climbing the ladder in the way you were supposed to.

When you first think of "Renegade," you think of bikers ... tough people with chains and beards.

You think of outcasts. Scalawags. Villains. People

not welcome in polite company.

Well, I hate to break it to you, but it's true.

As a business owner and entrepreneur, you ARE different from the average person.

You aren't a civilian expecting a paycheck at the end of the week regardless of whether you were productive. You really do understand that there must be productivity, there has to be profit, that you have to be in charge of your own life.

Renegade Millionaires are different and everybody who picks up this book with the dream of making way more money faster than they ever before believed possible has decided to embrace that difference.

To think differently. Act differently. To be willing to leave civilian life behind—with its corporate ladders, "approved" certifications, and socially acceptable expectations when it comes to the financial rewards we expect, deserve, and earn.

## "YOU'RE EXACTLY WHERE YOU WANT TO BE"

You presently have a belief system—an interrelated set of beliefs that have been formed over a period of time, that governs your thinking about yourself … about business … about selling … about everything.

This belief system is responsible for whatever financial and lifestyle condition you're now in.

In other words, *you are where your belief system determined you had to be.*

The first time I heard this concept, I wasn't very receptive to it. In fact, if there hadn't been several hundred witnesses in the audience, I might have gone up on the stage and strangled the speaker who said:

**"You're exactly where you want to be."**

At that time, I was driving a 1960 Chevrolet Impala bought for fifty dollars—on payments. Needless to say, it was not 1960. With ten dollars left to my name after having paid the admission to the seminar, the other aspects of life weren't in much better condition than the car.

And this idiot was saying, "You're exactly where you wanted to be."

It took a while for me to fully understand that it was my thinking, governed by my belief system, that had gotten me to that point. **And the good news was that by making changes in my thinking, through changing my belief system, I could change my circumstances.**

When we talk about money, success, and business, you have an already formed belief system about all that too. Some portions of this belief system are consciously known to you, others are not; they are the exclusive property of your subconscious mind.

But the beliefs are there, in great quantity and complexity.

And they are responsible for your present financial and lifestyle condition.

When we begin to examine the kind of thinking that goes with becoming a Renegade Millionaire, some of this thinking will be contradictory to your belief system. This is to be expected. (If your thinking is already perfectly matched, you probably wouldn't have purchased this book.)

Your belief system will want to reject these new and different ideas. Your belief system will tell you that these ideas are incorrect, unrealistic, simplistic, immoral, risky, or okay for others who are younger, older, better educated—but not for you.

As you work at understanding Renegade Millionaire thinking and mindset, you will be at odds with your belief system.

It's up to you to exert enough positive pressure to change what must be changed.

Throughout our lives, if our belief system does change (as in shifting from liberal to conservative), typically it takes place slowly, gradually, imperceptibly, as a result of maturity, experience, education, and the influence of others. Most of the time, the change is more by accident than purposeful intent.

What we want to do, though, in becoming a Renegade Millionaire, is to create that system of belief—that system of thinking—*and make those changes quickly, by design and intent.*

## NO FLUFF, NO THEORY, NO BS

This book assembles the most important observations from over four decades of work, consultations, and real-world experience—including but not limited to private individual clients, mastermind associates, and other coaching members.

It's all practical, rubber-meets-road kind of material and it's affirmed by the real-life experiences of well over 150 first-generation from scratch, entrepreneurial millionaires and multimillionaires.

And let me dissect that for a moment.

- **First-generation** means not having inherited wealth from others. I mean starting out in their businesses and in most cases their present businesses with at best modest resources, but in many cases with negative bank balances—building the business, not buying it.

- **Entrepreneur** means the individual built and controls and runs the businesses. I did not, for example, draw much in this program from corporate executives who merely implement strategies they have been handed from others.

Finally, everything you'll discover inside the pages of this book can be applied by anyone willing to put in the effort to become a Renegade Millionaire.

In essence, you are getting over $100 million worth of entrepreneurial street smarts channeled through these pages.

## WHAT IS BEING A RENEGADE MILLIONAIRE ALL ABOUT?

It's about making a decision—here and now—to embrace reinventing your business, uncovering and tapping into undiscovered sources of money inside your business, accelerating your level of productivity …

And finally …

Having the freedom, autonomy, and wealth to live life on your own terms.

That to me is the whole thing.

So instead of fighting this notion and label of "Renegade," we have to embrace it. Be happy with it. Revel in it.

Really be honest with yourself.

"This is who I am and how I'm going to live."

Now let's proceed.

## The More Entrepreneurial You Are, and the More Successful You Are, the Fewer Groups You Can Possibly Fit Into

I've had many mentors, coaches, and instructors in my life. I wouldn't be where I am or enjoy the life I am blessed to live without them.

What I really wanted was to be able to understand how Dan Kennedy thought. ***And the best place for that amazing display was the Titanium mastermind group—the mastermind that had launched so many other successful businessmen and women throughout the years.***

I can't come close to laying out the many Renegade Millionaire lessons that I learned from Dan, but here are a few of the key ones:

**Time Management**: Dan wrote the book(s) on this one. When he worked, he worked. His time was scheduled in strict twenty-minute blocks, and he never deviated. Discipline. Getting things done without distraction. Focus.

**Rules of Engagement**: Train people how to engage you or you will forever be beholden to others' agendas. "Their emergency is not my emergency." Dan does not own a cell phone. He does not email. He has no FB, Twitter, Instagram, or Snapchat account to communicate with him in any way other than pre-scheduled private client calls.

**Authenticity**: Dan tells it like it is. He doesn't hide anything. His entrepreneurial journey began at a very early age. He openly admits where he failed (testing), made poor decisions (being human), or dealt with severe setbacks (part of life). No excuses. You pull yourself up by the bootstraps and get back in the game.

**Autonomy**: This one is huge. Dan taught me not to care what others thought. Dan values his time over money or materialism. He flies in a private jet because it saves him time and hassle. He makes his clients fly to Cleveland to have consulting days with him. Dan understands positioning and value, along with scarcity.

**When in Doubt, Don't Follow the Majority**: Dan taught me to question everything and everyone (the opposite of my formal school years, which was pretty much memorize and regurgitate). It took me years with Dan and one other significant mentor to reverse years of educational brainwashing.

**The Wealthy Get Paid in Advance—the Poor Get Paid in Arrears**: Think about that one. How many people provide services today and wait to get paid, send an invoice later, carry financing, or "wait for insurance to pay."

**Business**: You're not in the business of xyz, you're in the business of marketing xyz. You may offer a superior product or service, but if you can't market effectively, you will hit the ceiling on your income and business value. There's no real value in "things" (or services); the real value is in selling "things" (or services).

**Sloth/Laziness**: Dan despises sloth of any kind. Personal or business. Zero tolerance. Our new age entitlement society drives him crazy.

***"There are many reasons to be poor in America, but there are no good reasons to stay poor."***

*Continued on page 18.*

# WELCOME TO THE MONEY PYRAMID

Shown on the following page is the basic ***Money Pyramid***.

The money pyramid has not changed one iota in nearly seven decades—specifically, since 1954, which is when coincidentally the Social Security Administration started to track where people wound up after forty years of work.

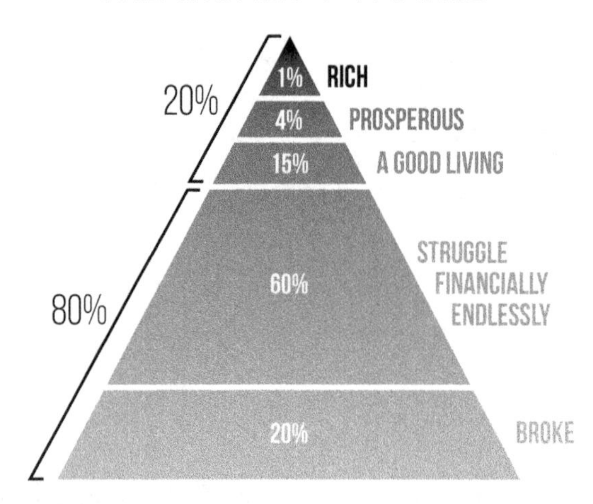


Times change. Governments change. Economies change.

The Money Pyramid doesn't change.

Here's the reality it so starkly reveals—in any population of business owners / entrepreneurs, the statistics for success inevitably break down as follows:

**20% are broke.**

**60% will struggle financially … forever…**

**15% will make a good living**

**4% will become prosperous**

**1% will become RICH**

Only 1 percent achieve riches. These are the evil 1 percenters we will always have with us.

By and large 20 percent of the people can manage to finish out their lives without making a choice between their Alzheimer drugs and their dog food.

When you drop down below the top 20 percent, that starts to change radically—and whether they own their own business, work in some kind of career, or struggle to get by doing whatever they can, that's the remaining 80 percent of humanity.

So note again: only 5 percent really are living and experiencing anything close to what most would consider a successful, prosperous kind of lifestyle.

Now you might be asking yourself, "Okay, so what am I to take away from this statistic?"

The answer is a clear understanding of a key Renegade Millionaire principle:

**"The majority is always WRONG."**

Looking at this pyramid, it's pretty clear that a full 95 percent of people, therefore, are totally, absolutely 100 percent wrong about their entire approach to life … certainly about money, but it's hard to argue if you wind up at age sixty-five dead broke, that you did much of anything right.

Now you may have been a good person; this is not any kind of conversation about morality, it's totally about the level of functionality.

When you go in any population, anything you carve out … Cleveland, it's the same as the national population. If you go to millionaires, it's the same, 1 percent of them really got their act together, another 4 percent are kicking ass and taking names, and then it starts to disintegrate dramatically.

I promise you this is true.

This is everywhere, I don't care how you create a population:

- if you take all the dentists in North Dakota
- if you take all the dentists who do Invisalign
- if you take all the lawyers
- if you take all the personal injury lawyers
- if you take all the personal injury lawyers who are Catholics …

It's all the same, it doesn't matter.

You're going to find this same darn pyramid.

And from a money standpoint, think about everything that's changed since 1954 that should have affected this.

Just think of access to information; if you don't know how to change a lightbulb, there's a YouTube video on your phone to teach you how to change a lightbulb.

And there's one to teach you how to do pretty much anything else. You don't have to go get a book; you don't even have to be able to read, the darn thing will tell you, *"A tablespoon of this, a teaspoon of that."*

You don't have to go to the library ever if you don't want to, it's on your phone.

All this is accessible. Any idiot can make stuff and sell it on eBay or Amazon.

*All of the excuses to be broke are gone.*

I've never yet met a broke person who doesn't know how to make something. They can knit, they can paint, they can cobble stuff together with wood and nails, they all know how to make something.

Every broke person I've ever met, they know how to make stuff that somebody will buy.

But before, they had to figure that stuff out, "Oh, where am I going to go sell it? How am I going to get a store to sell it for me? I can't get to the swap meet because I don't have a car."

There were a lot of barriers to knitting a sweater and selling it. All those barriers are gone, you don't have to leave your house except to ship it, and you don't even have to do that; they'll come get it at the house. You don't even have to leave.

*And yet, the stats never change—same darned pyramid.*

This is the first thing you've got to get; it's hard for people to get. They recognize it over here, but they don't recognize it over there.

But every time I'm with any group, I'm thinking 95 percent of these people are clueless—which means, I can't go looking to them for wisdom, strategies, advice, and support.

Instead, I've got to find the 5 percent; then I'd REALLY like to find the 1 percent.

But Renegade Millionaire 101 says if I can't find out who the 5 percent are, and if I can't find the 1 percent, I can at least *not do anything I see the other 95 percent doing.*

No matter how rational it may appear, I know it isn't, because of these statistics.

So this is an all-in kind of deal; these stats are universal, they apply everywhere to every group you belong to, every population you're a part of, every place you go.

These stats apply to everything you do and it boils down to this:

**You have to NOT behave like the 95 percenters.**

You can't afford it, not if you want to be at the top of that pyramid ... which is where you'll find Renegade Millionaires.

*Continued from page 10, from Renegade Millionaire Dr. David Phelps*

Three keys to a successful business that Dan taught me:

- **Price elasticity**—There is no restriction on what people will pay, only self-imposed limits. Most people undervalue themselves, their services and products, poorly package or differentiate from commoditization and underestimate what the market will pay.
- **Transaction size**—Revenue benchmarks can be created by different pricing structures. It requires fewer $10,000 sales than $1,000 sales to reach a million dollars, but it is not proportionately more challenging to create and sell a $10,000 thing than a $1,000 thing.
- **Continuity or subscription revenue vs. transactional income**—The world of education is built on being a better and more efficient "doer" of whatever thing you train to do. Instead, strive to create continuity income streams where you do the work once and have a customer for months or years, or best, a lifetime.

"Time waits for no one." Do what you need to do, say what you need to say and do it now. Don't wait. You can't buy back time, not even with all of the money in the world.

**Dr. David Phelps**
*Freedom Founders*

# WHAT IS A "RENEGADE MILLIONAIRE"?

When was the last time you thought of yourself as someone who throws the typical and conventional to the wayside and not only pushes the envelope, but practically shreds the darn thing, to live and experience life where few are willing to go?

That, in a nutshell, is what it means to be a "Renegade Millionaire."

If you just break up the language, the **RENEGADE** part of it gets to being a contrarian. It means being willing to do everything differently, violate all of your industry norms, and annoy your peers—and often industry regulatory bodies—while you do it.

It means being viewed as this sort of odd, weird, unpleasant somebody … who is ALL ABOUT RESULTS.

The **MILLIONAIRE** part basically speaks for itself.

But it's more than just the number, because obviously a million doesn't mean the same as it used to.

What it really means is that you are out-earning your norms and you are out-net-worthing your industry norms.

## THE CORE PREMISES OF BEING A RENEGADE MILLIONAIRE

### 1. The Majority Is Always Wrong.

We've touched on this already and I'm sure you see that this explains a great deal about how we get the elected officials that we do. (Although, just imagine who we'd get if we actually had a majority of the population voting.)

There's 1 percent of the US population that gets rich and 4 percent that achieves financial security and independence while 95 percent don't. So that tells you that 95 percent of the people around you have the wrong thinking about money, and about success in a broader sense, about business, about advertising, and about marketing. Otherwise, if they were right, all those percentages would be flipped around. So the statistics tell us this.

Even so …

*It's still very hard to look at all the people who we grew up with—our school teachers, our family, or our employees whom we've been working with for ten or twelve years—and come to the conclusion that 95 percent of them must be disregarded and can't be listened to, that they're all wrong.*

But that is, in fact, the case.

One of the early greats in the motivational and self-help field, Earl Nightingale, used to say that:

- If you don't know how to do what you need to do to get where it is you want to go …
- And you don't have anybody around who is

your model or your mentor or who has legitimacy, who has traveled the path you want to travel and arrived at the destination you want to arrive at …

- Then what you do is look around at what everyone else is doing …
- And DON'T do it.

That's your starting point.

So the first premise is to look at what everybody else is doing, strip away everything because you recognize that the majority is wrong, and then take a minority viewpoint by doing the exact opposite.

### 2. Breakthroughs Come from Outside a Business, Not Inside.

So again, most people get into a business and they're adaptive to how things get done around here … essentially, they're sort of Amish-like in that they operate in a closed community.

Take the professional speaking business as an example.

Somebody sees a "successful" speaker and says to them, "I really want to do what you do. How do I do that?"

Well, if for no other reason than ease of giving a short answer rather than a long answer, what almost every speaker does is say, "*Well, you should join the National Speakers Association.*"

So now they join an association, which in that industry has only one trade association. Then they go to that industry's convention. They now surround themselves with a circle of people already in that business. And everything now becomes incestuous, because they're only looking at what everybody else is doing.

Everybody in every industry does exactly the same thing.

If they're in the insurance industry they hang out with insurance guys. They read sales books written by insurance guys. They go to the insurance industry association convention. They only read the insurance industry trade journal.

Trouble is, the only kind of improvement you

can make in this scenario is at best incremental. No breakthroughs can come from that because no one's even trying to have a breakthrough. Instead, everybody's just trying to do what everybody else is doing, only trying to do it just a little bit better.

So the SECOND premise is **breakthroughs come from outside, not inside**.

### 3. Marketing IS Your Business

Renegade Millionaires understand that marketing your business is the most interesting, enjoyable, fun part of the business ... and in fact—**MARKETING is your business.**

Most people, if you ask them to describe what they do, will state it in a very narrow sort of shopkeeper terminology.

So, if we go over here to the neighborhood jewelry store and ask, "What do you do?" the guy first of all will look at us like we're idiots, but then he'll say, "I'm a jeweler."

If he's a little bit more business-minded he might say, "I own a jewelry store."

We go next door to the people that have a little ice cream shop to ask the same question. They'll say, "We'll, you're in an ice cream shop."

That's really how most people think. If you ask them at a cocktail party, you'll get the exact same answer.

Renegade Millionaires understand that we're in the MARKETING BUSINESS. The thing or things we choose to market are ancillary to the marketing. Everybody else thinks the marketing is ancillary to the thing or things that they do.

Again, this is 180 degrees out of sync with how most business owners think.

Everybody thinks the thing they DO is the business. But it's not.

**The MARKETING is the business.**

If you go to a chiropractic convention, the cocktail conversation will be about technique, whether you use the activator gun, yadda, yadda, yadda. Same with realtors, insurance agents, speakers, florists, whatever. They will view advertising, marketing, and sales as either ancillary or a necessary evil.

Everybody sees things this way.

Renegade Millionaires learn to flip that equation.

We view MARKETING as the business we're in and the thing we do as ancillary.

Ultimately, that viewpoint leads to being our greatest core competency, our greatest skill, as well as our greatest interest and enthusiasm—the thing we have fun with—the marketing.

Which is really EMPOWERING because once you can market one thing effectively, you can market anything effectively.

### 4. Use ONLY Direct Response Advertising.

Renegade Millionaires fully embrace direct response advertising—this is the first thing you have to embrace. If you don't embrace it, all you're going to do with your advertising money is flush it down the toilet.

You've got to stop listening to the people saying: "*Get your name out there.*"

The only businesses that kind of marketing works for are the ones who have unlimited budgets like Coca-Cola or something similar.

STOP thinking about getting name recognition, image, brand, visibility, exposure. These are the false gods worshipped by most advertisers.

Your goal must be RESPONSE.

And how do you accomplish this?

**By only doing advertising deliberately designed to leap out from its cluttered environment and grab its intended audience by the throat and force them to pay attention.**

A Renegade Millionaire will pretty much use any device or means necessary to do just that.

Renegade Millionaire marketing is 100 percent opposite of anything you've been programmed to do by the media or education.

Remember: the majority is always wrong. When you realize that most of the advertising you see is from big, dumb companies, that should tell you something.

In contrast, direct response offers you the only

scientific approach to advertising—where you can track every dollar invested to see every dollar returned and everything can be measured.

When you spend a dollar to drive traffic to a website or a phone number or a door, you can measure what kind of return on that investment you obtained. Then you can make changes to your marketing based on whether you got a good return on that investment dollar or a bad return on that investment dollar.

There's nothing emotional about it. Test to see what works. Use the one that works. Throw out ones that don't. Simple. Effective. Disciplined.

And Renegade Millionaire marketers are extremely disciplined.

### 5. Your Wealth Is in Your Customer List

Renegade Millionaires come in all styles, shapes, and sizes and arrive at their ultimate place of success through many different paths of thinking and discovery.

But one thing all Renegade Millionaires DO have in common is this:

- A relentless focus on building up our list of customers, which we sometimes call our "herd"—because we recognize that all the real wealth is in the herd.

Again, by *herd* I mean the constituency, the audience, the group of customers or clients or patients who can be retained by you, and who have the ability and the willingness to give you money repetitively, over and over and over again.

So, let's take the independent restaurant owner. His wealth is not predicated on whether he owns his own restaurant—the wealth's not in the building, the wealth's not in the kitchen, the wealth's not in the secret recipes on the computer, the wealth's not in the location, the wealth's not in the insanely great five-year lease he has.

The wealth is in the customers.

And that's the ONLY place there is any real wealth.

Therefore, that mandates how you spend your advertising and marketing dollars.

For example, if I own a restaurant, I don't want

to spend money to advertise my restaurant anywhere that does NOT also have mechanisms in it to collect names and addresses and phone numbers and emails of people who might be interested in coming to my restaurant.

Because the herd is worth more than anything else.

When you say that, the average person does not understand that concept at all—they're clueless.

And a lot of people have very high-income businesses for a number of years, but wind up where they started in terms of wealth because current income tends to get spent immediately and they never invest in creating, growing, and nurturing the herd.

So the smartest thing to do with ALL your advertising is have it work to attract ONLY the appropriate person for what it is that you do. Never spend a dollar that does not directly do that.

## IMPORTANT: THE REAL PURPOSE OF MAKING SALES

Most salespeople think the purpose of getting a customer is to make a sale.

Renegade Millionaires think differently—the purpose of making a sale is to get a customer.

Why?

The ONLY real asset that matters to your business is an actual customer and the relationship you have with that customer. Because all other assets come and go and are vulnerable—subject to a loss of value and essentially have no value without the customer.

Your customers and the relationship you have with them are the one asset you can have in your business that can make it possible for you to literally create income at will. John Lennon of The Beatles once said, *"Whenever we want another swimming pool, I sit down and write a song."*

What he really meant was that whenever we want anything—another mansion, to pay alimony, whatever we want to do—we create a song. But that's incomplete because the song is worthless if there aren't a million fans out there lusting after and waiting for the next song they can buy the minute it exists.

Now very few of us have that kind of talent—to write a song or great American novel. Very few have that. But we can put ourselves into John Lennon's position by creating the other side of that equation: the herd, the group of customers whom we have carefully rounded up, put a fence around, taken care of, nurtured a relationship with—done all those things so they're there waiting for whatever we come up with next.

That's why you work so hard at making sales to get customers ... you're not after that one-time transaction, you're looking to create a relationship that provides value over the long term.

---

### 6. Reject All Limitations

Many business owners have a belief system about how they (and the opportunities offered by their businesses) are limited in one way, shape, or form.

By the way, they all think it's unique—if they were just in some other business, they wouldn't have this problem.

The LEGAL stuff they often refer to involves compliance, so the lawyers will tell you about all the stuff they can't do, by law. "We can't do that."

First thing a financial person will tell you is, "We can't use testimonials."

(Note: There are sixteen different ways they can legally use testimonials. Even registered investment advisors can use testimonials, but they will immediately tell you, "We can't. No, no, no. We can't use that.")

About 50 percent of the refunds over the years of the now famous Magnetic Marketing System were due to self-imposed limitations. "I'm a [fill in the blank] and we can't use any of this by law."

What you will find if you probe is something

that looks like this:

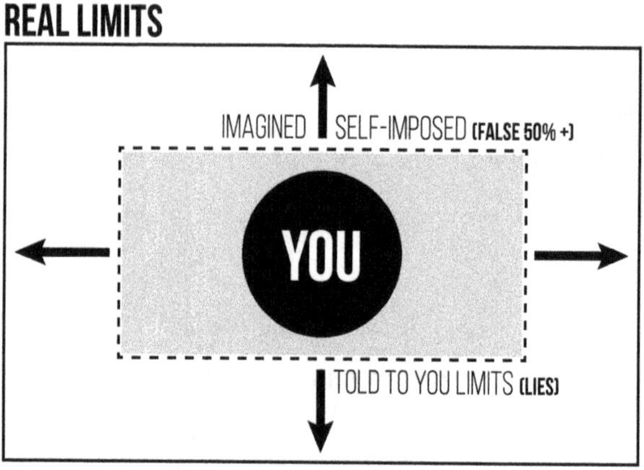

REAL LIMITS

IMAGINED SELF-IMPOSED (FALSE 50% +)

YOU

TOLD TO YOU LIMITS (LIES)

You will find inside this diagram that YES, there is indeed a real limit somewhere.

There's actually a law about what they can and cannot do, and it may be an industry law, a professional law, a Federal Trade Commission law, an FDA law, an SEC law, the law of gravity, the law of God, whatever. There's actually a real limit.

Then they have this box they've made of the limits they believe in.

And there's this giant gap in between the two.

Mostly, they're in love with that dotted line. They sleep with it every night. They whisper sweet nothings to it. They believe in it like they believe their religion.

They HATE being disabused of this, in part because they've been conforming to it for so long and comforting themselves with it as the EXCUSE they're not doing any better.

Price is a perfect example. They will quote to me a variety of real limiting things about price, like, "We can't sell for that price because we've got fifty-six competitors within walking distance. Same stuff we sell is sold on Amazon. We have a dwindling number of customers."

They've got all kinds of reasons and excuses to defend their self-imposed limit about what they can and can't do with pricing.

This goes on constantly, and every time you hear it from yourself or from anybody else, you hear a dotted line verbally described. "No, we can't do that because …"

You've got to be smart enough to instantly

recognize what it is.

It's somebody's dotted line.

That's what it is.

There is a real limit somewhere, but it's a long way away from the dotted line, and what Renegade Millionaires do is they understand this. They recognize it.

And they simply don't accept it anymore.

# 7 SECRETS TO EXTREME WEALTH, AUTONOMY, AND ENTREPRENEURIAL SUCCESS

## Renegade Millionaires Make Sales to Create Customers, Not to Make a Sale

Dan's books sit on the shelf right behind my desk where they are dog-eared and post-it-noted from years of reference and implementation.

Dan changed how I thought about not only marketing, but about creating long-lasting relationships with my clients—relationships that were mutually encouraging and supportive, with clients achieving outcomes beyond what they imagined possible.

Dan said often (and I'm paraphrasing), ***"You can get a customer to make a sale or you can make a sale and create a customer relationship for life."***

He changed my entire attitude toward money, sales, wealth, time management, people management, and so much more.

Because of Dan, while raising teenagers, I put a sign on my door and it read, "***If you are bleeding, call 911.***" It didn't last long on the door but no one ever interrupted me again when I was working.

Dan showed me the power of a clear client avatar, a clear marketing message, a clear offer, clear pricing, and clear delivery.

Most of all, he showed me that boundaries and limits are the mark of the truly compassionate and mature businessperson.

**Baeth Davis**

*YourPurpose.com*

# SECRET #1—THE POWER OF ORGANIZED EFFORT

Most peoples' effort is NOT organized around any strict governance, organizing theory of business, philosophy or ethic, definite plan, none of that. Most effort is unmoored, reactive, and random. People and businesses easily lose their way.

Most of that effort—particularly in regard to marketing—is what I would call random and erratic acts of marketing. Their lives really are random and erratic acts, largely reactive and not very predictive.

Even when something is clearly predictive, procrastination about the soon-to-arrive debacle makes it show up as if you never could've predicted it in the first place.

For example:

QUESTION: If you've got "one," what's going to happen at some point?

ANSWER: Whatever that "one" thing is, it's going to turn to crap.

One way or another—whatever it is, one account, one client, one employee, one source of business, one source of traffic, one source of whatever—if it's got the number one in it, you can predict with 100 percent accuracy in advance that it's going to turn to crap, eventually.

99 percent of people never prepare for it. They just wait until it happens.

In contrast, Renegade Millionaires approach every day, every challenge relying on a pre-developed system of organized effort that stays consistent with a set of guiding principles.

This is what says yes or no to the constant stream of questions, strategic decisions, problems, solutions, opportunities, everything that the entrepreneur must manage.

MOST PEOPLE are using tactics in search of a strategy.

Only those who are more sophisticated are using *strategies in search of principle.*

We're all guilty of this.

If we're not really conscious of this danger and we're not extremely careful, this is how we do most of everything we do—both in business and in life.

Why?

Because no one's naturally inclined to pursue some kind of organized, methodical effort to get from point A to point B.

Instead, the more natural response is: "This happened and now I've got to do something about it."

We react. And not only that, we often just react with a ***partial piece*** of something; we don't even do a ***complete*** thing in response.

The answer to this is to have in place "Governing Principles."

## PRINCIPLES ➔ STRATEGIES ➔ TACTICS

The way business should work is you start with a governing principle.

Then you translate that principle into strategy.

Then you figure out what tactics to apply to implement the strategy. (Preferably all at one time.)

Principle should be locked in place as governance.

Strategies make the principle practical and actionable—and are flexible.

Tactics represent the implementation of strategy—and are flexible and situational.

- PRINCIPLE is King.
- STRATEGIES are the King's Leadership Council.
- TACTICS are the Foot Soldiers.

Most people start with tactics; most people are very tactical. Kid won't clean his room, what are we going to do to get the kid to clean his room?

Stop. Think. Go all the way back to principle.

What is the principle here about how we want the household to work?

What is the principle about how we want the relationship with the kid to work?

Then and only then do we ask …

What are the strategies? What are the tactics?

You actually could've prepared for the kid not cleaning his room, but instead there was no preparation. We waited until it happened and then we find ourselves painfully engaged in random and erratic tactical behavior.

And then we wonder why the room is still a mess.

## THE POWER OF GOVERNING PRINCIPLES

So, when you analyze businesses and the way businesspeople behave, you will see that the Renegades, the 1 percent, the top performers, they have this little list of governing principles for almost everything.

If you think about Disney, their governing principle above everything else is this:

**"The Happiest Place on Earth."**

It's not just a slogan. It is a statement of their governing principle.

Now that causes all sorts of strategic choices of what they're going to do on a day-to-day basis. They've got to have strategies to have people leave feeling like they were at the happiest place on earth.

Now there's some stuff they can't change. Guests are going to stand in long lines in sweltering heat with unhappy children, but they can do something. They can:

- Make standing in line entertaining with interactive displays, story elements, even "Hidden Mickeys."
- Offer three different ways to buy your way to privilege to shorten the line.
- Send people to run around on the worst days with spray bottles with propellers and spray water on you and play with you and make like it's a game.
- Do all kinds of other stuff to try—strategically and tactically—to get to this governing

principle.

Ask yourself: What's the governing principle? What are the strategies? And then finally, what are the tactics? This is a way of thinking you don't often see.

## EXAMPLE: HOW TO THINK ABOUT "FOLLOW UP"

Let's say your business's Governing Principle is this:

> *"No Fail Follow Up: We Will Leave No Lead Behind."*

That may or may not be the right thing to do by the way, but if it is, then we need to figure out a strategy to put it to work for our business.

For example, I would ask the financial advisors in our Renegade Millionaire Mastermind group:

> *"What do you do about all the old people who come to your dog-and-pony show dinners who don't book appointments?"*

Remember, these are professionals making half a

million dollars a year; they're intelligent, they're not stupid. They understand the value of a lead.

So—here are the THREE things they told me they do:

1. The real honest ones said, "We don't do anything."

2. The other ones said, "Well, if Helen has time, we have her call them." Does Helen ever have time? Of course not, because Helen doesn't want to call them. Helen will create fires to put out rather than make these calls. She's not going to call anybody.

3. "Well, we dump them back in the email and mailing list." And what do they get then? Three months later they get an invitation to the same thing they were just at where they didn't book an appointment. How stupid is that?

*"Well, that's what we do."*

Remember, all making half a million bucks a year—and now we know those are the three things

NOT to do.

We can throw those "tactics" out and we can start to have a real conversation about how to organize this effort to make sure "*No Lead Gets Left Behind.*"

For example:

- Create an "appointment-no-sale" sequence ... where we send them the same offer, then a price drop offer after that, with a different offer behind that.
- Flip the tele-reps—so if Barbara talked to them and couldn't close them, we have Susan talk to them.
- Create a new special event we can invite them to attend.
- Exchange and sell the unconverted leads with someone else, so we actually cut our lead cost in half or down to a third or down to a fourth.
- Send them a completely different offer with its own complete sequence.
- Look at the system we're using to manage

> follow up—are we using something like Snappy Kraken or are we doing this with pink slips and file folders?

THAT is how you get down to a granular level on the tactics used.

THAT is how you create an ORGANIZED EFFORT rather than a purely random, erratic act of marketing.

## HAVE A COMMITMENT TO WHAT WORKS

Bill Clinton once said that he went to sleep one night as the young punk in the room that nobody wanted to listen to, and he woke up the next morning as the old fart in the room that nobody wanted to listen to, and he couldn't figure out what happened in between.

There are always these false choices that people make in business of "It's either this, or it's that."

The latest being it's either the new media and new technology or it's the old.

You should be agnostic about almost everything and ONLY interested in WHAT WORKS.

Recognize that what works in your thing may not work in his thing or a different mix of things may be appropriate. Use whatever is available in order to get the results you want in advertising, marketing, selling, and in business.

We make these false divides all the time and what we should focus on instead is what works … new, old, whatever.

Mostly the new is really an evolution of the old anyway.

Craigslist is classified ads from newspapers and magazines. Live webinars and video sales letter (VSL) is the new TV infomercial. I've moved the work I did in the old infomercial environment over to the newer webinar and VSL environment. What is now a VSL online used to be sent out on a DVD—and it still works on a darn DVD sent to somebody.

The desire and tendency to walk away from "what was" in favor of "what now is" is a mistake.

For example, there's the CD/DVD argument.

*"Why on earth are we still doing DVDs and sending them out? Nobody even has a DVD*

*player or CD player anymore."*

Here's an example from one of the most successful home improvement direct marketers on earth. It's called SunSetter Awnings and their entire pitch is an Idea Kit and DVD.

You fill out a card to get a FREE Idea Kit and DVD. I'm sure by now they've added a website, but you're getting a free DVD.

You might say to yourself, "Well, that's because they're selling to a bunch of old farts." But they're not. Their homeowner demo is right at age forty; it's not age fifty and sixty. This is their control piece.

These people aren't stupid. Wouldn't they rather

be all digital? Yes, you bet they would. But this isn't the control for nothing.

The idea that this is OLD, this is NEW, we want to only use NEW, and we want to only use OLD, is a very, very bad idea. It has never really been totally true.

Media particularly takes a long time to die. People think it's going to die long before it really does.

So—don't run after false choices. Commit to what works. True Renegade Millionaires are like me—they are agnostic. They like facts. They have information. They have empirical evidence and they have no preconceived preference for where it ultimately leads.

The ones who harm themselves and block opportunity have a preconceived preference for where things lead and then they are picking and choosing based on that preconceived preference.

For example, say you write books. A lot of books. And you don't like Amazon being in the used book business. They divert a new book buyer to a used book buyer. You don't get any royalties on the second sale of the same book, the third sale, the fourth sale, the fifth sale. The only people making money are Amazon.

But this isn't going to go away. And it actually sells a lot of books to people who wouldn't buy books otherwise.

So now the pragmatist would ask, "How do we jerry-rig the book in such a way that we make sure it leads to us?"—such as inserting offers for other stuff like lead magnets and so on.

This is what being an agnostic pragmatist Renegade Millionaire is all about.

It doesn't matter if we like it.

It doesn't matter if we approve of it.

The only thing that matters is our commitment to what works.

## Renegade Millionaires Re-Invent

My first introduction to the Magnetic Marketing community and Dan Kennedy was when I read my first book written by you, *No B.S. Business Success*. I had been in business for about four years, and we were going through a particularly difficult time. It was the middle of the recession. ***We were broke and I felt hopeless and discouraged***.

The second-to-last chapter of the book is about how to get a business out of trouble. In it, you relate your experiences with failures, crushing debt, and trying to just make it to the next day.

You said that in business, we all make mistakes and screw up, whether our fault or not. There is no time for shame. ***That the only shame is in giving up without a fight***. When I read those words, the weight of my discouragement felt lighter, and my hopelessness less threatening. Maybe that's why it's such a vivid memory.

You also related a time when you faced a potentially devastating failure. ***It forced you to come up with a solution that wasn't your Plan A, but your Plan B was actually superior***. You wouldn't have known it if Plan A hadn't failed.

Those words and lessons were embedded in me. And it made my failures less traumatic. I've learned over the years that ***fear of failure is the biggest obstacle that prevents success***. The words I read that night gave me boldness to take risks and not be afraid. Otherwise, I would have given up long ago.

You also talked about business re-invention. ***You said that if your***

***business is failing, direct all your energy into re-inventing your business***. The next day, I took a notebook and wrote the words RE-INVENT on it. I divided the notebook into two sections.

In the first section, I wrote down all of the ideas and lessons I was learning. In the second section, I wrote my action plans and tasks that I was going to do. I also created a folder in my computer called REINVENT for all the new marketing I was creating. It was a reminder of my goals for this business.

**My marketing folder is still called REINVENT to this day.**

If I had to choose one word for you, it would be "overcomer." You overcame poverty growing up, you overcame the lack of a college education, you overcame stuttering, you overcame alcoholism, you overcame a fear of public speaking, you overcame rejection and ridicule for being a contrarian. And likely many other things, personal and professional, that only you know about.

**Kia Arian**
*Zinegraphics.com*

---

# SECRET #2—MAKE MAXIMUM MONEY

This shouldn't be a surprise or controversial, yet most businesspeople are not as focused on this as you might think they would be.

Entrepreneurs are not focused on this—they are CONFUSED about the purpose of business and about their own responsibility—and confused people are dangerous to themselves and to others. They get distracted from making money by many divergent sirens and activities, such as:

- Fads. Peer pressure. Ego.
- Habits. Fears. Social pressure.

- What somebody or everybody else is doing—without any data or facts on whether it's actually making money.

THE relevant question to ask yourself with any activity:

**"Is THIS making money?"**

Non-adherence to this principle produces all sorts of bad strategy and, in turn, tactical mistakes.

For example, democratizing employee compensation (as opposed to "spoils to the winners"); incurring extra time, energy, or financial costs to try and appease and keep all/worst customers—vs. let 'em go. A timid pricing strategy where you're always afraid to raise prices.

The word MAXIMUM is important here—nothing lasts forever. There is no permanence or certainty in business.

Renegade Millionaires are VERY focused on making maximum money. But this perspective is truly uncommon, particularly for the whole "be your own boss" crowd—it's the furthest thing from their mind.

If you sell to businesspeople, it's critical to understand this point.

The overwhelming majority of the "be your own boss" crowd are in business for other reasons than to make maximum money. They're in business to have something to do ... they like animals, so they became a veterinarian ... they're honestly a little teed off that they have to climb down into the mire to muck up their hands with all the business stuff at all.

The "be your own boss" crowd especially wants nothing to do with business; they just want to do what their job was and not have a boss.

A car mechanic opens a shop ... he didn't open a shop to make money; he opened a shop because he didn't want a boss.

So, if you're trying to sell him something that would help his "BUSINESS" and not have anything to do with crawling under a car with a grease gun, you're going to only make him mad. That's not what he's interested in.

Now he might tell you, "Of course I want to make a lot of money." But he's not going to invest the level of time, energy, or thought into exactly what that will mean for how he runs his business or what it will take to actually make that happen.

Very few businesspeople think about how to make maximum money ... instead, they stop way short of all the detail that could produce maximum money in their business.

For example, here's how I approached this back when I was speaking on the Peter Lowe SUCCESS tour. There was a twenty-two-point list of things to do to extract the maximum money from each speaking opportunity, which took place over nine years—it was a big tour that involved twenty-five to twenty-eight gigs per year. I won't go into everything on this list, but here are a few key items:

- **Negotiate the highest percentage**. In a speaking arrangement, it's all about splits between the event producer and the speaker. As a speaker, I got 60 percent of every sale made, giving 40 percent back to the producer.

Most of the other speakers had it the other way around or at best 50-50.

- **Process the orders and credit cards.** I was the only one to process my own orders because everybody's lazy, they just let the producer handle it. Then, after several weeks passed, they'd get a check in the mail. Except for me, I took the order forms, processed them, and sent THEM a check.
- **Sell at a higher price than the others**. The house wants everyone to sell lower-priced programs, so they get higher sales volume. Why not set your price to make as much money as you can from every gig?
- **Have an order form that gets handed out and SELLS.** Make sure the order form gets handed out to the crowd every time. Put sales copy on the form itself to help secure the sale as well as collect information.
- **Give audience members a reason to stay**. Provide an extra handout and message to

get people to stay and hear you speak: "10 Reasons to Stay & Hear Dan"—as the last guy on deck and not the big name that got them there (e.g., Colin Powell, President George H. W. Bush, etc.). Do whatever to keep them in their seats so they'd be there to listen and to buy.

- **Confirm that "Stick" letters got out the NEXT day to every sale made**—put a stopper on refunds right off the bat.
- **Follow up on non-buyers with direct-mail/ sales letter.** Why leave money on the table? The money was more than made back on that follow-up sequence, even with giving the house a generous share for the privilege of using their list.
- **Use dead time productively.** Get every dollar you can get out of the trip. For example, if switching gates between planes you could meet someone (back before TSA)—nowadays, at least you can schedule a

sales call, write a letter, something other than just wander through the airport.

*Most people do NOT think this way.*

If you asked any of the other speakers on the tour to show you their list of twenty-odd ways to make maximum money from the gig, they'd give you a blank stare like you were from some other planet or something.

But the 1 percent crowd—Renegade Millionaires—think like this.

## THE WRONG AND RIGHT WAY TO DOUBLE YOUR INCOME

The all-time champion of worst idea for doubling your income is to double your work.

You'll be a rich corpse.

This is also the most unimaginative, uncreative, non-analytical approach.

Consider farmers. At one time they all plowed with mules. They tried to get the mules to pull harder, move faster. They hitched two, three, or four mules together. Then tractors. Then faster tractors. All the same brute force multiplied.

In contrast …

One of my earliest consulting clients in the 1970s was a company that did very complex, detailed soil analysis of farms. Their sales rep collected soil samples in test tubes from every part of the farm. In the lab, they analyzed each sample. On a color-coded map, they depicted nutrient and mineral deficiencies—different in soil only a few feet away from another hunk of ground.

They prescribed different fertilizers for different parts of the farm. The soil's ability to produce was greatly multiplied. Not by the farmer working longer hours, not by more mules pulling harder, not by a bigger tractor.

By scientifically, strategically, cleverly leveraging the real asset: the soil.

Now consider salespeople. To increase income, they will try to generate more leads, squeeze in more presentations, run more appointments, work longer hours, talk on the cell phone while driving, eating, even while peeing!

But that's not leveraging the real assets: time and sales skill.

Consider the business owner. Same approach. More advertising, more leads, more customers, more products, longer hours.

It is all too common to attempt reaching bigger financial goals simplistically, by adding more customers to beget more sales even if you must personally work more hours and juggle more responsibility and absorb more stress, and add more overhead.

But this IS simplistic. Almost unthinking. Certainly uncreative.

A more creative, cerebral, interesting approach is to *search for ways to achieve more with less.*

## THE POWER OF LEVERAGE

Let's talk a little bit about leverage. The thing about leverage is it's very hard to make a lot of money without it.

Our tax structure here in the US—which is very

unlikely to change—makes it almost impossible to get really rich purely from earned income. Like Chris Farley, you would have to live in a trailer down by the river and keep all the money. Even then, it's doubtful.

So you have to think in terms of income and equity to leverage within a business and leverage outside a business.

How do we make it do more than its core?

It goes back to those twenty-plus things we laid out to get the very most opportunity out of every speech.

You ask yourself, "What are the things we can do to get more out of this business?"

Here are some points of leverage to consider:

### Multiple Uses for the Same Assets

One is to look for multiple uses for the same assets or units of work.

So, whatever the unit of work is inside your business, how can you get more than one payday for it?

Inside the information business, it's obvious. Do the seminar, record the seminar, sell the seminar long after it's over to people who weren't in attendance.

But you have to ask yourself this about everything you do and with every customer every time they come and go through your place of business.

Steve Adams did a great job with this in his retail pet stores by ramping up and promoting the service aspect of the business. He told me that just in pet washing, they did $50,000 per store times forty-two stores. Why don't the other pet stores do it? "Because we're not in that business. We want people to come, pick up dog food, and get their tails out of here."

No. We want them to come, bring the dog, stay as long as they'll stay. We want them getting the dog washed. We want them getting the dog trained.

So, what is Steve doing instead?

He's getting multiple value out of the same customer.

Here's a story about visiting Disney World and Epcot.

I walked into the Norway store, more accurately the Norway/Frozen store. In one part of the store they have a large display of hand and body lotion—

on the label it says *Frozen* from the movie.

*Frozen* hand and body lotion, a little bottle of it, is $40. Think about that. Probably $1-2 to make it, including glop, bottle, and color label. $40 retail.

Now, as I'm wandering the park, I'm paying closer attention.

In the regular gift shop, there's Minnie Mouse hand lotion. It's only $10 because it's not as popular, but it's the same glop, I promise you.

I found twenty different ones as I walked around, all different prices based on the popularity of a label on the bottle of glop. In fact, there's no claim even for the glop—there's not like a little sign that tells you the glop is made from whizz-bang leaves from the papaya tree or something.

None of that. There's just *Frozen* lotion at $40 a pop. Minnie Mouse, $10. The one with some other princess on it, $12.50. Always the same glop.

As soon as Disney discovered they could sell hand and body lotion, they said, "How many characters have we got? How can we take the same glop, same bottles, and change the label? If we don't sell enough of this one, we'll peel off the label and put another one on."

That's leverage inside the business.

## Create Equity

Here are two writer-downers.

- The value of a business rises with continuous or continuity income versus episodic or transactional income. Two businesses, same amount of revenue, same profit, but the one that has continuous or continuity income is more valuable than the one that has episodic or transactional revenue.
- The value of a business rises as customer lifespan increases—same revenue, same profit, but the business that keeps the customer for the longest span of time has the greater value.

So, you need to forget income and instead think about "How do I create equity inside my business? How do I increase its value?"

### Current Bank vs. Future Bank

This is an extremely important concept to grasp.

Most businesses focus on making deposits into their Current Bank.

Renegade Millionaires make sure to put energy into creating deposits for "Future Bank."

- *Current Bank* is the money you make today.
- *Future Bank* is the money you count on making based on strategic decisions and actions.

Here's a real-world example that should make this very clear.

If you ask a restaurant owner, "How was your weekend?"—mostly he's going to answer you with a number or numbers related to Current Bank. He's going to answer you with how much revenue he did or how many tables he turned. Those are going to be his two answers.

A Renegade Millionaire is going to give you some kind of "Future Bank" number, which in the restaurant business is names, addresses, phone numbers, and birthdays.

They will know how many data cards they collected, because the birthday is future money. Almost everyone goes out to a restaurant to celebrate their birthday. Few go out to eat for their birthday alone. Most people go with at least one other person. Many go with two other people or more.

So, if I'm in the restaurant business and I have your contact file, and I have your birthdate, and I have your spouse's birthdate and kid's birthdate, I have money in my "future bank" if I wisely use it.

And I don't have to be a marketing rocket scientist to cash the check—all I have to do is send out a card with some kind of offer to entice you to come in to redeem it.

And you can track how many of those cards translate into dollars—and thus every birthday you collect, you can extrapolate with a decent level of precision just how much money you've just deposited into your Future Bank account.

## THE UNCOMFORTABLE REASON WHY SOME MAKE MORE THAN OTHERS

Here's the often discomforting reality about why people get paid what they get paid.

Typically, the more they get, the less it has to do with what they do, and therefore comparatively how well they do it.

And even though you might think it depends on the quality of product or services provided, it just does not have much to do with the deliverables.

This is very disconcerting to people who are really into their deliverables.

A guy that has a shoe parlor on one side of the street actually makes pretty good shoes.

A guy with a shoe store on the other side of the street is selling junk that was made in China and is put together with glue, and he doesn't care about the quality of the shoe one way or the other.

But the second guy makes a lot more money. (I'll tell you why in a second.)

Doesn't matter—shoes, healthcare, home repair, whatever—businesspeople think that the comparative differential quality of the deliverable is what should drive demand and their compensation.

It doesn't. Not even close.

As uncomfortable as it is, the thing to get and the thing to remember that you won't like, and that most of your peers would hate and would never admit, is this reality:

The higher up the monetary food chain we go in our compensation and the nature of the people from whom we get it, *the more we are paid for WHO we are and WHO we are perceived to be by them, than we are paid for WHAT we do.*

But nobody wants to accept that—and even if they do, it's like pulling teeth to have them embrace it to the degree that they actually start using it as a strategy to raise their level of income.

Perfect case in point:

In our herd, there's a Money Under Management Advisor for people who've sold companies for $20 million or more. Let's call him Ted. And Ted has a perfect package of stories for that audience.

His life story is terrific, his childhood story is

terrific, his current charitable activity story is terrific, and Ted is perfect for them. He's like Will Rogers, Andy Griffith in *Mayberry*, Longmire on that TV show. He's that guy.

But everybody around him on a day-to-day basis keeps trying to make him talk about what he does and show pie charts.

It's a constant, uphill battle to get him to burn the pie charts, to stop talking about the Fed, to stop talking about diversified, derivative, portfolio stuff.

What he needs to talk about instead 24/7 is TED …

He should talk about how he grew up using outdoor plumbing, how he was the first person in his family who went to college, selling stuff door to door when he was twelve to pay for his own clothes …

They should see Ted on video at the ranch house in Wyoming with a cow wandering around, and a ukulele leaned against the rail and a tin cup in his hand.

That's what Ted's talking about, not wealth management and Goldman Sachs.

Forget about pictures and videos of Ted with books behind him. Every financial advisor (and lawyer) does that. They've all got the same books.

Forget the books Ted, show us you and a cow.

It's so hard for people to get this and they fall back away from it.

If you've got credentials you worked really hard to get, you want to believe that's the thing. If you've got an alphabet soup of letters after your name, you want to believe that is important.

But it's WHO you are perceived to be.

AFFINITY matters more than CREDIBILITY.

STORY matters more than FACTS.

All the differentiation is in who we are.

You should know, I personally hate this. I do not like it. I have made my peace with it, but I don't like it. I would like to make all my money with nobody knowing anything about me.

That would be terrific. I hate all of this. I used to hate it and had not made my peace with it. Now, I've made my peace with it, but I don't like it.

So, this is not about me telling you something

that is my preferred and favored business model. It isn't. It just happens to be the one that works best.

There's a difference, for example, between Dan at let's say $100,000 for a marketing project and somebody at $10,000. There is a skill level; there is an experience level, there is a difference. It is not a 10x difference; it ain't that big. It might be two on average. But Dan charges 10x.

How can you charge 10x for something that is only really a 2x?

It's this:

*It's who you are perceived to be by the people you do business with, not what you do.*

Why people get paid is really important to get a grip on, and it is totally different than what 99.9 percent of people believe about why people get money.

## In Four Weeks from a $1 Book To $15,000 Mastermind

I Google-searched Dan Kennedy and ordered your one-dollar book offer. The book was *No B.S. Direct Response Marketing for Non-Direct Marketing Businesses.*

One phone call later in the week I was on with one of the Magnetic Marketing team members. I spent $2,000 on Ultimate Marketing Machine and Magnetic Marketing.

I watched those videos and ***two days later I got on the phone again and asked to take the $2,000 I had just spent and put it towards the Platinum Mastermind with you guys.***

In less than four weeks, I went from a $1 book order to a $15,000 Mastermind. ***That's how positive I was that your teachings were right for me.***

I started to consume every piece of content you had ever created. I would listen to your seminars for five or six hours a day, I read all of your *No B.S.* books and I flew over to meet you in Orlando for SuperConference.

The way I think now is so heavily influenced by what you taught that I can not even differentiate your teaching from my original thoughts … and in two years of learning from you I was able to leave my job safely and securely without risk of where money was going to come from.

***I've become a #1 best-selling author, built a podcast and have***

***interviewed billionaires (borrowed trust), run a website with nearly 100,000 readers a month, and have positioned myself as one of the five most famous and influential people in my niche.***

I have regular clients who pay $400 an hour to speak to me, and I am signing companies every week that are paying me $20,000 to $30,000 a year to market for them.

And you know what, I am having a crap ton of fun at the same time. I love what I do, and I am really good at it, because of you!

**Mikkel Thorup**

# SECRET #3—THE POWER OF BIG IDEAS

This is really a pretty simple concept, and it shouldn't be shocking, yet people forget it.

With most really great businesses, the ones that rise to the top of the heap, you'll find one key thing about them that you do not find with a lot of other businesses.

There's at least one, radical, BIG IDEA.

It's easy to overlook and even forget, especially if any time whatsoever has passed since the origin of the company and its current state of success. Often, without that history, what was indeed radical at its time is no longer radical and doesn't seem all that radical to us.

So it's useful when you see highly successful individuals or highly successful businesses that you think are potentially worth modeling to look at their history to see just how radical those ideas were ten years ago, twenty years ago, whenever it was they made their play—especially if that notion has now become commonplace.

## WHERE BIG IDEAS ARE BORN ...

There are three simple strategies common to many BIG ideas:

- violate industry norms
- appeal to malcontents
- be a true leader and not just an alternative

Let me give you a couple of examples.

Way before YouTube and the internet there was a generation of highly successful professional comedians ... and this was before the comedy club circuit really came into being.

But these comedians created the comedy club industry due to the strength of their own popularity. Guys opened clubs because if you booked one of these guys (like Bob Newhart), people came.

The business doesn't work that way now, but if you went and looked back at that ten-year period of time, ask yourself, "What triggered that?"

It was because a handful of radicals defied industry norms AND became true leaders—*by agreeing to make comedy records.*

We don't think anything of that now, because comedians can be seen on TV, on YouTube, you can get MP3 downloads—it's all out there in the marketplace.

At that time, the record companies went to guys like Newhart and they wanted to do this. But everybody else was terrified, because, "If people can hear our act, they won't want to come see us and we make our living in Vegas and Atlantic City, in New York and LA," where there were comedy clubs. "We'll kill our careers with this."

Making a record with your act on it was a radical, big idea, and in the entire first three years of this experiment, there were fewer than twelve comedians who dared to do it.

It literally made them the superstar money-earners of the tribe of their time with this incredibly strange, scary idea.

*Newhart's first record knocked The Beatles out of the #1 spot* and he held it for sixteen months after ... with a comedy record that people sat around in their living room and watched turn while they listened to it.

This was this big, radical thing they did that almost nobody else did or was willing to do for quite some time.

I'll give you a big, radical idea of mine from back when I was primarily in the speaking business:

**I decided to be a farmer, not a pirate.**

This was a big, radical idea and it's still a minority position within the speaking community. But I went that direction because I quickly figured out that speaking was a crappy business. At its best, it's a high-paying job, but it ain't a business.

It's great media—and it may well be the best media of all—as long as you don't mind going and doing it. Because not only don't you have to pay anything for it, for many speaking engagements, they pay you to go get a basket of customers. There's no other media that does that.

But speakers in my time, they were all pirates:

- We leave the cave;
- We plunder;
- We bring it back to the cave.

If we have staff, we divide it up with the staff. We keep what's left and then we go plunder again.

That's the pirate business model.

Everybody who was in that ten-year window ahead of me, whose names you would know, who came up with me, those that are still around are still playing pirate. And given the challenges of filling rooms, most of them are having to sail the ship farther to ever more distant shores to go play.

That's the problem with being a pirate—one day, there might not be any treasure left.

I became a farmer instead and used it to grow things that I kept and still have value.

Here's the proof to that pudding.

When I speak at an event like SuperConference or Growth Summit, I'll ask the audience:

> *"Raise your hand if your relationship with me began by being in an audience where I spoke somewhere? Now keep your hands up if it's been five years or longer that you've been with me. Okay, ten years. Fifteen years. Now put them back up if you think you've spent over $100,000 total … on me, with Magnetic Marketing, everything …"*

Hands rise and stay up all around the room.

It all came from that source.

It all happened because I switched to farming.

This is an example of a big, and at its time, certainly radical idea.

Now how does this get applied on an ongoing basis?

Well, even when I couldn't afford it, when I was flat broke, I turned down speaking engagements when the audience didn't fit my target customer profile (entrepreneurs and business owners). If I went and spoke to a group of schoolteachers, I wouldn't have any success harvesting them as customers that would be giving me money ten years later. So, I wouldn't take the speaking gig to schoolteachers, even though it might have paid me very well.

Everybody else, all the pirates, they would go anywhere for any price to any audience that would have them. That's how you must operate if you are a pirate. "I don't care that they're a bunch of electrical engineers who will never spend a penny with me again, I'll still come."

I did that once and realized, "Wrong audience. Wrong people."

Never again. Done pirating. I don't get to farm there. I don't go if I can't farm.

You will find this kind of big, radical idea behind every big success if you look hard enough. And you shouldn't settle for NOT seeing it if you're going to model something you think is successful, because I'm certain it is hidden there somewhere.

## THE BEST BUSINESSES ARE ABOUT SOMETHING

The best businesses are always about something in addition to making money—at least in the minds of their patrons. Besides commerce, great businesses tend to be about something, some grand idea, mission, positioning, philosophy, something that everybody can hook onto.

The strategies to making this happen involve things like:

- maintaining consistency with governing principles
- creating "deeper-meanings" relationships with customers
- evangelism, not just patronage

This is an important factor to consider even within the context of making maximum money.

Sometimes businesses lose touch with this as they grow, expand, age, are bought and sold … you no longer see what made them work and made them great.

That's why the study of history is vital—it's a hazard the Renegade Millionaire knows to guard against.

The businesses that really go off the rails after once having achieved serious success are almost never due to market conditions changing and producing a fatal blow.

Typically, businesses go off the rails because they lose sight of that special something, chickening out about standing for something specific and unique, and instead just becoming about commerce and transactions.

And then they go into the death spiral.

## ANTI-TIMIDITY STRATEGIES

First of all, only sell stuff you
actually think is great.

Then, when you sell it, you don't have an internal reason to be timid. There truly is a whole lot of stuff to sell.

You don't need to stay in a business that you don't feel great about.

Understand what really works and do it.

The standard should be, what gets us the best result? Period. If we are ostracized by our peer community, we can make new friends. You can get a dog. You can round up homeless people; they will applaud you.

You don't need a peer community. There are lots of people on the planet. If you make a lot of money, you can buy friends. They will hang around you; they will walk behind you and clap for you if that's what you want them to do.

But do what works. Get your own ego out of the way.

### If you pick an anti-establishment audience, keep bashing the establishment.

Most of my money has actually been made going into environments where there is an establishment to poke hard and irritate and annoy and cause them to intensely dislike me. And there's a bunch of people waiting who were thinking the same thing but haven't voiced it and they rise up and attach to it like there's no tomorrow.

Again, you have to be willing to be the person that, as you walk through the room, a bunch of people turn their back on and walk over to the other side.

You have to be okay with that if you are going to play this game.

### Bottom Line:

Big ideas work—especially if you truly believe in them and have a thick enough skin to stay the course.

# Masterminds Were Imperative for My Growth

I attended my first Dan Kennedy Magnetic Marketing conference in November of 2014. I took seventy pages of notes. Dan really opened my mind to so many marketing concepts and changed the way I market my business forever.

The first thing I did was write my first mini-book for a recruiting business I had at the time. It's still the first thing I do when I start a new business or roll out a new service. I just wrote one a couple of weeks ago.

The second thing was to learn that good is good enough. I got a hundred times more done because I wasn't waiting around for things to be just right to get to the next step.

I knew about overcoming objections and calls to action on sales calls, but I had no idea about how to sell one to many from the stage or from a sales letter.

Masterminds are imperative for growth. I wasn't a millionaire so I wasn't in his group but I did join two of the other masterminds and learned so much through the other members and the hot seats.

The art of pricing, bonuses, creating urgency ... he was amazing. I had no idea how to close a bunch of people at once but with his techniques, I did it twice from the stage at one of his conferences. I wrote two courses, something I'd never do without the education I got from him.

Buy his books and courses and you'll see.

I'd still just be cold calling and suffering through one-on-one appointments as my bread and butter if it weren't for him and his team.

**Erica DelSignore**

***PerfectLegalVideo.com***

# CHAPTER 6

## SECRET #4—TAKE CONTROL OF YOUR TIME, YOUR BUSINESS, AND YOUR LIFE

Here's the critical reality to grasp …

When the Big Guy kills your clock and they start closing the lid on your coffin, there'll be money left over, but there won't be any time left over.

Go ahead, steal my money.

I can replace the money.

Steal my time?

But of course, you know, this means war … because I can't replace the time.

Most people think the opposite. They think,

"My money is my most valuable thing, but heck, I've got lots of time." They have elaborate locks and security systems and cages at the business to protect their assets and inventory.

But do they have similar locks and security in place to keep people from stealing their time?

Not a chance.

We go to great extremes to protect our stuff. We pay premiums on insurance to protect our stuff. We're real big on our stuff. But most people have no protections in place whatsoever to safeguard their time. They let people drop in whenever they want. Phone rings, they answer it. Email/social media/internet ... all day long the interruptions keep coming.

There's nothing safeguarding their time at all.

All that stuff is readily replaceable, just as the money that bought it is readily replaceable.

Renegade Millionaires have come to grips with just how easy money is to replace, but how hard time is to replace.

## THE VALUE YOU PUT ON TIME DETERMINES YOUR INCOME

Time is predictive. I can predict … based on how effectively I used my time today, what my bank balance is going to look like next week, next month, and next year.

So, it's something that I can measure, monitor, and exercise control over daily, rather than play catch up when I get "after the fact" reports and try to fix problems after they've occurred.

How you value time is a great acid test of integrity.

An instructive example is Bill Clinton, who was legendary for starting meetings whenever he showed up, not when they were scheduled.

I use it as a test to determine who I'm going to do business with. I'm pretty ruthless about NOT doing business with people who demonstrate that they have real problems with time.

On the other hand, Renegade Millionaires are very, very good at this—far better than the average business owner and especially the average person on the street.

And quite frankly, you know, there's a correlation between the value they put on punctuality and respect for time to what's showing up inside their bank balances.

Along with a healthy RESPECT for time, there are also keys to using this resource effectively.

The basis of this isn't the old saw re: "time management"—which by itself isn't a bad thing by any means—instead it's based on this key strategy:

## Never. Ever. Ever. Ever. Start from Scratch.

Entrepreneurs have a burning desire to create and invent stuff. Many would prefer to reinvent the wheel when the wheel already in the garage is perfectly okay.

Not that everything's already been invented, but there's often no real payoff in doing invention for invention's sake. In fact, there's a real danger to inventing in your business when it's not necessary.

For example, in advertising and in marketing we recycle all the time. Of course, people will say, "Let's come up with something really new this time for this campaign."

And I'll say, "Well, the trashcan mailer works great, let's use it again."

"But you've used the trashcan mailer eighteen times this year for eighteen clients."

"Yeah. Because it works. So, let's use it again."

Remember: Time is your most perishable, irreplaceable asset and MUST be treated as such in every way possible—which means don't start from scratch when there are assets available to get you traction quickly.

There's a history for almost everything. Everything you see now is a rehash or a hybrid of something that went before, which means there's a rehash or a hybrid for you to use—so you never have a blank page of any kind.

It's horribly time-inefficient to start from scratch and time is the most perishable asset we have.

Again—you can replace anything else. You can

replace people. You can replace money. You can replace stuff.

But you can't get that hour back. You can't do it.

So, never start from scratch. Understand when you look at things and you see them, think about, "What am I seeing that didn't start from scratch?"

For example—Elon Musk. What is Elon Musk when we look at Elon Musk? He's two things. Thomas Edison and P.T. Barnum. There's nothing new there. There's a hybrid of Thomas Edison and P.T. Barnum.

If you want to be the next Elon Musk, understand that's what you're seeing.

Jeff Bezos manages like Jack Welch and he's built monopolies like the robber barons of the industrial age. That's what he's doing. You want to study them if that's what you want to be.

HBO has remade *The Sopranos* more times than you or I can count. All they're doing is changing the costumes. One show after another, it's in old England, it's in medieval France, it's *The Sopranos* again and again. They've got a template now.

It works. Just do it over and over again.

Disney's using the same Walt story template. The same one. They didn't change crap, and the few times they've gone away from it, they've dragged themselves back.

Starbucks, it's a European coffee joint.

Craigslist, it's what used to be the classified ads section of your newspaper.

So never start with a blank slate.

## A LESSON FROM DISNEY ...

Here's a little-known Disney story about that blank slate.

In the early 1990s, a group of Disney writers proposed something that had never been done at Disney before. These guys wanted to do an animated movie based on an original concept written from scratch. Never been done at Disney before, Disney uses fairytales that already existed.

The studio chief at the time was Jeffrey Katzenberg, a twenty-nine-year-old. He was extremely skeptical, but he let them go pitch the idea to Michael

Eisner who was CEO at the time.

In the meeting with Eisner, the pitch goes nowhere—it's a complicated, multi-generational story set in an exotic location … told by animals … all imagined from scratch.

Groping for a reference, Eisner says, "Can it be King Lear with animals?" Because everybody wants some kind of "tastes like chicken" reference.

Somebody in the group says, "No, but I think it could be Hamlet. We could do Hamlet."

The film won two Oscars and a Golden Globe. It was the highest grossing film of 1994. By 2014 it had earned over $1 billion. It's still generating money today—live action version, Broadway play, TV stuff on the Disney Channel, merchandise, on and on.

It's *The Lion King*, but it had never been done before.

Contrary to myth, it wasn't original at all. It was Hamlet with lions. They gave everybody a thing they could hang onto. It got made when it wouldn't have been made had it stayed a blank slate.

*It exists because somebody found a way not to make*

*it start from scratch.*

A great lesson for us all.

## THINK LIKE A PARASITE

One of the most effective ways to save time and money—specifically related to the energy and expense it takes to acquire customers—is to form alliances with other businesses who serve your market.

We sometimes jokingly refer to this as becoming "a parasite." The connotation is negative, but what you're doing isn't negative for anyone at all.

It can be a huge amount of work to create customers from scratch and to make a market, when it would be *infinitely easier and quicker* (and in many cases, less costly and more profitable) to be a parasite on some other host and to get the customers they have already organized and to feed off of the market they have already made.

Now, in truth, everybody does it to some degree. They just don't do it because they don't think of it in these terms consciously.

For example, when you go speak to the national association of whatever and you sell product and acquire customers, you're a parasite, they're the host.

Look—they've already put together a market, right? And you're now coming in, feeding off it.

If you advertise in a magazine, they're a host, you're a parasite—because again they assembled a market and you're feeding off of the market that they put together when you rent a list.

Etc. Etc. Etc.

Let's take this a step further into the world of joint ventures and strategic alliances.

Entrepreneurs have established a market. By that I mean they have influence over customers who have a willingness and ability to consume. If they are aggressive and progressive and so forth, the problem they very well may have is that they simply can't keep pace with the demand for new products from that herd.

They need product.

If you have product but don't have customers, this is a match made in heaven.

And if you have product and you have tested,

proven marketing that works, it's truly a match made in heaven.

Renegade Millionaires understand this and, in some cases, launch businesses by being parasites. Pretty soon, they're able to play both sides of the fence—helping out others when THEY need product to deliver.

People mess it up when they don't make it brain-dead easy, simple, and painless for the person they want the access and cooperation from to say YES.

Remember—the last thing they want is more work. They've got all the work they need. So, if you've got a product, but can't effectively market it, you're doomed. I don't care how good the product is because that means they've got to do the marketing for you.

That's a NO GO.

Instead, you go in with a package of every component part necessary to implement the deal—with tools and support and everything they need to make this work already done and ready to go in the can.

Most people don't approach joint ventures that way.

Another thing most don't understand is that people who are doing well ... naturally and understandably, grow risk averse.

So, when you come to them with something new and you want access to their customers, if they have any brains, they're just as interested in safety as they are in the money.

And so you have to address the safety issues involved in the deal, like "how can I be sure that your thing actually works, you've got marketing ready, your tech won't crash, that you'll actually fulfill it," and on and on.

They'll want to see some kind of history that will put them at ease.

Most people are not prepared in that way.

## SAVE TIME USING OPR

If you take the textbook/business school approach, you would believe that the path to entrepreneurial success is:

Step 1: IDEA

Step 2: RAISE OR BORROW MONEY

Step 3: DO BUSINESS

That was the Dotcom approach, right? Create an idea, go get Other People's Money (OPM), cash out in an IPO (Initial Public Offering).

More like, raise money, spend money, go out of business.

Not a good model.

Lots of people still think OPM remains a necessary component part of creating and building a business.

I think it's actually destructive. Instead, Renegade Millionaires often think in terms of Other People's Resources (OPR).

A number of our top Magnetic Marketing Members who have launched new businesses within their businesses, they've done it all via host/parasite relationships, usually a joint venture with another Member and the business is created and it is profitable.

And nobody ever put any money in.

## FORGET INVENTION—START RE-USING

It's important to realize that fortunes continue to be created without invention—by just re-using ideas and business models that have proven successful already.

The restaurant industry thrives with drive-through windows, which they did not create. And now drive-through windows have proliferated in all sorts of other kinds of businesses: drugstores, dry cleaners, sports betting, even weddings.

The mechanism of "continuity" started way back in the book business and the "book-of-the-month" club.

We now have fruit of the month, cheese of the month, underwear of the month, pet toy of the month, you name it, on and on.

Layaway plans were originally created by banks. They were called Christmas clubs where you made deposits all year long to save the money necessary to buy presents in December.

And then layaway spread to stores. They called them layaway plans. You could buy the item today; the store will hold it for you while you make little payments every week or every month until you've paid for it in full and then the store gives it to you. They do this now in all kinds of businesses, even funerals.

The idea of a "gift with purchase" is usually credited to Estee Lauder in the cosmetics business. Well, now everyone in the information business uses a gift with purchase. Everybody in the automobile business uses a gift with purchase. Most industries have businesses that use a gift with purchase.

Renegade Millionaires avoid invention from scratch because it's expensive, messy, and time consuming. As you learned earlier in this book, your time is more valuable than anything else.

Rather than INVENT, Renegade Millionaires tend to adapt, model, reuse, and repurpose.

That's where fortunes can be made as quickly as possible.

And speaking of that …

## MONEY LOVES SPEED

Renegade Millionaires understand that money is attracted to speed. They do whatever they can to shorten the time between an idea and the actual appearance and introduction of that idea into the market—where it can be offered and sold.

There's very little value in going through endless exercises to create detailed plans, specifications, focus groups, and so on. With the rise of the internet and always-on-demand services, the software industry has realized this and gone from what they used to call "the waterfall method" of project management, where everything is laid out in copious detail before a single line of code was written, to a methodology known as "agile"—which relies on quick bursts of activity to get "something" out the door and into the marketplace.

This isn't new. Way back in the dark ages when Lee Iacocca was running Chrysler, he realized the company was bleeding cash from every pore and something had to be done to fix the situation.

Iacocca was down on the factory floor one day walking around and one of the factory workers says to him, "That car over there would make a really cool convertible."

Iacocca says, "Yeah? Get a blowtorch." They cut the roof off one of the cars and he then says, "Let's go drive around town down by the college and see if girls look at it."

That was the extent of the research … no long design process … no specifications … no focus groups. Just a blowtorch.

Then Iacocca, the factory worker who came up with the idea, and an engineer drive into Ann Arbor, Michigan and bop around the college campus and the bars and stuff. They stop at traffic lights. They pull into parking lots to see what happens.

What happens?

Girls come over and look at the car.

They drive back to the factory and Iacocca says, "We're making convertibles."

THIS is how success happens.

It's starting things before you're ready to do them.

The flip side of that is not only starting, but having a massive sense of URGENCY in actually getting it done and out to market.

One of the biggest differences between Renegade Millionaires and everyone else is their sense of urgency. Ordinary folks, like the ones who work for you as employees or vendors, their sense of urgency on a one-to-ten scale is about zero and a half.

It really doesn't matter to them whether it happens today, tomorrow, next week … and they don't respond even to problems in their own lives with any sense of urgency.

The less invention you do the faster you can move. You can invent if you have the luxury to do so, but you may never even want to invent.

Time is of the essence. Get to the money.

## You Are Truly the Millionaire Maker!

I first heard of you early on when I started my chiropractic practice in 2004.

I was not any good at marketing (as most aren't in the beginning) but became fascinated with (and obsessed with) it after reading just one of your newsletters.

1. You helped me to have the confidence that I needed to become successful in business. I listened to the "How to Have Unstoppable Confidence" audio CDs over and over, to and from work to really work on my mindset. You made it possible for me to get where I am today.

   I was a shy, unconfident introvert who couldn't close a deal to save my life. Your sales book specifically changed my ability to sell. Every concept from Apples to Oranges, to Selling Money at a Discount ... every single concept was so big for me.

2. Your NO B.S. Magnetic Marketing group in Columbus was the place where I sharpened my teeth on my marketing and advertising skills.

3. ***I was able to grow and sell my chiropractic business by using the business and marketing concepts that you taught me; you truly are THE MILLIONAIRE MAKER.***

   I could never have imagined the success I have had for my family and me before I landed on Planet Dan!

4. I have been able to meet so many of my best friends through your events and have been able to have such great teachers

in the ***mastermind groups like Peak Performers and the Renegade Millionaire Mastermind.***

5. I had a hard time believing "The Phenomenon" (achieving more in twelve months than you did in the previous twelve years) was possible when I attended the conference in Orlando. ***I am having my phenomenon year THIS YEAR with the sale of two businesses, and several ventures I've set up so I am the TOLL BOOTH just as you taught!***

**Scot Gray**
*StemCellFinder.com*

---

**READY TO BECOME THE NEXT RENEGADE MILLIONAIRE?**

Check Out Our Complimentary
Renegade Millionaire Marketing Assessment at
WWW.RENEGADEMILLIONAIRE.COM/BOOK

## SECRET #5—ACCURATE THINKING

Let's start talking about what I think could be the most important secret of all and that is accurate thinking.

Note that I didn't use the term "intelligence" or "smarts" or "wisdom" here.

I used "accurate" as in "knowing facts you may not want to know."

This matters because we all have a tendency NOT to want to know a lot of stuff that's actually going on.

Most people just recoil in horror from accurate thinking about the reality of human beings, human nature, and businesses.

I once had a client who was the reigning expert in America in retail theft control for convenience stores and supermarkets—learned a lot from him … for example, most store owners believe the major "loss" problem is due to shoplifting.

Wrong. Their losses are not from shoplifting. They have them, but the overwhelming cause of the loss is employee and delivery person theft.

He had catalogued 132 ways that employees steal and 71 ways that delivery people steal. He was a delivery thief at one point in his life, so he knew from personal experience.

In the supermarket industry, shoplifting accounts for 3X the owner's net profit … which means employee and delivery man thieves are making three times what the owner's making from the business—with no investment, no regulatory compliance, no insurance, no nothing.

The owner takes home $1 and the thieves take $3. Of course, there are no taxes on theft, so really, it's an even bigger spread if you want to make yourself feel worse about it if you're the owner.

But … and here's the kicker …

*Almost no empirical evidence shown to store owners convinces them that THIS is the problem.*

They really have to be beat up to buy it and do anything about it.

## A WORLD OF SITUATIONAL ETHICS

It boils down to the fact that there's about 5 percent of humans who will always do the right thing no matter what. That 5 percent of the population is hard-wired so that they cannot lie, cheat, steal, or any of its equivalents. If they're starving and a loaf of bread falls off a truck as it goes around the corner, they'll pick up the loaf of bread and chase the truck to the next traffic light to give the driver the loaf of bread back. This is how they behave.

That's 5 percent of humanity. They can't help themselves.

Then there's 5 percent who lie, cheat, steal, and all the equivalents all the time, no matter whether it benefits them or not. This is how they are hardwired; they cannot help themselves. They haven't told the truth since they were three years old.

Now understand, theft isn't just "I grabbed twelve bottles of water to resell to my neighbors out of my garage and do this with every convenience store I deliver to."

There is also time theft, non-compliance with your sales scripts, your procedures, your programs. They're all a form of lying, cheating, stealing, etc. etc. etc.—it's a very broad issue.

In between those two extremes of the 5 percenters are where you and I and almost everybody else live. We have situational ethics, meaning our lines move and adjust based on the circumstances that we're in.

It's important to know this about people.

Accurate thinking demands it.

For example, let's say you're at the supermarket and you get out to your car and you discover the cashier gave you ten dollars too much change. Most everybody takes that ten dollars back in, right?

But I could start to chip away at that:

- it's pouring down rain;
- you had to park five miles away from the store;
- you've got your kids with you and one of them has peed their pants;
- you promised to pick up your spouse at a certain time, and they will be standing out in the rain, and you are late;
- and the cashier was mean to you, they put the eggs on the bottom beneath the watermelon and it's already leaking through the paper bag.

At some point, I can tip almost everybody to saying, "Screw it. The ten bucks is staying in my pocket," and off you go.

Since you can be tipped, you and anyone else in that 90 percent category could be tipped about anything.

That is the accurate level of thinking that's

important to know.

Now, other than the 5 percent on the fringes, this is NOT about good person/bad person, this is about all persons. All of us.

If you don't want theft happening inside your business, then you must control the only things you can control … and that's *the ability to operate under the radar and undetected.*

That's the only thing you can control. That's it.

This is not about trust, it's about "trust but verify."

Inaccurate thinking is, "Oh no, he would never do that to me because we've been buddies for thirty years now." We all believe what we want to believe. We project onto other people all sorts of fundamentally inaccurate beliefs and desires and motivations that are not real.

We are consistently disappointed and then we do it all over again.

We do this with all kinds of things, not just people.

Have you ever driven an old car when you didn't

have money? I've got money now, but I'm back to old cars. It's amazing. But you project—will it start? We don't know. Will it run? We don't know. What did you do every morning when you cranked that key? You talked to it, "Come on baby, one more time …"

We project onto it what we WANT it to be, despite what we know intellectually.

You know intellectually that thing is a hunk of metal with problems and talking to it won't make a damn bit of difference. But you did it anyway, didn't you? We all did.

This is the number one way business people cause problems for themselves. We project onto people, customers, clients, patients, associates, partners, employees, and even things.

We project onto situations how we want them to be.

We have a lot of reasons why we do this, even when we know it is factually inaccurate. We somehow believe that this time, it WILL be accurate. For us. This time. This person is different. This situation is different. This thing is different.

No. It's not.

When I say they will all go lame, they will all go lame.

Wait long enough and they will all go lame.

They're great until they're not.

That is accurate thinking. It's hard, I know.

But Renegade Millionaires don't run from it, they embrace it.

## LITMUS TESTS AND OBSTACLE COURSES

In various ways, we make lousy investments in other people—which drain our power; drain us financially and emotionally; drain our time and energy.

The same thing occurs in regards to a business or opportunity we get involved with.

This needs to be avoided and prevented not by wishing, but by establishing rules and litmus tests.

Every successful Renegade Millionaire I know uses litmus tests when choosing whether to kick off or continue an association or relationship.

For me, one key litmus test is *punctuality*. My

theory is that if they can't or won't keep small commitments, it's pretty hopeless to think they're going to keep big and important ones.

There's also a **"Will They Work With You Again?"** litmus test. It's really very simple.

We're looking to do a deal together. Are there three people who've done deals with you more than once? Unless you've got three, the answer is no.

Why? Because I'm unlikely to be the first who has a great experience when nobody else has wanted to get back in bed with you a couple more times.

I know a number of people who in hiring have deliberately set litmus tests based on **whether the applicant can follow instructions**. They run a test. If they can't follow a simple set of instructions, it's pretty much a sure bet they won't be able to do so when it becomes really important.

Here's another tip that's a few years old, but it still holds up well … A guy won the lottery. But he waited to come forward until he had time to call everybody he knew and ask this question:

*"I need to borrow $1,000 right away, and I*

*can't tell you why I need it."*

This cut down dramatically the number of people who came forward after it became public knowledge that he'd won the lottery.

It's such a good tip. If you ever hit it big … you sell your company for $100 million … before you tell anyone, do something similar.

Another thing I like to do to safeguard myself is set up what I call an **obstacle course** for anyone coming to me for help, advice, money, whatever.

This boils down to seeing if they will do anything that demonstrates the necessary initiative, responsibility, resilience, persistence, whatever qualities you think they should have.

I've had relatives that wanted money from me for their business ventures. When I'm in their house, I look for the books they have that relate to this wonderful thing they want me to invest in … or at a minimum that show "I'm studying business."

No books. No money.

Say for example someone comes to you saying they want to start a restaurant. You could respond with something like this: "Fine. Here's what I'd like to know ..."

Then you give them the homework list.

> *"Here are the sixteen things I want you to go find out, get, take good notes, come back and tell me the market conditions in this town where you want to put this thing. The average home price, the demographics. Who else has a restaurant there? How many American Express cardholders are there in that town who regularly go to restaurants? I'm not going to tell you how to find out, but that information is readily available. Come back to me with that stuff and then we'll talk."*

That'll end 90 percent of it. They never bring it up again because they're not going to do that. If they did, by the way, you should be encouraged because it shows that they have at least a rudimentary, gut-level understanding of what it takes to succeed.

The more elaborate the obstacle course, the more

of them will go away.

You can regulate behavior—customer, client, patient, staff, family—by litmus tests and obstacle courses. Hardly anybody will go through much of an obstacle course to get whatever they came to you for—they just won't do it because only the top 5 percent on the Money Pyramid has the gumption.

## SAD BUT TRUE, IDIOTS EVERYWHERE

My big personal advice regarding accurate thinking is this:

*Act as if everybody you deal with is a dim-witted, distracted, utterly unreliable idiot.*

Every day you can be pleasantly surprised if you follow this methodology. If you don't follow this methodology, you are almost assured of some very disappointing days.

First of all, people forget their jobs every weekend. They report on Monday and they need orientation. It's just the way it is.

Here's an example.

Imagine you and I are having a conversation. We've been working together thirty years. You're smart, you're not an idiot. We have a conversation about one thing.

I need to paper trail it immediately.

"That conversation we had yesterday, here's what we agreed to. You will wear a tie and meet me for dinner."

If I don't paper trail it, I am going to be disappointed.

Now, will you be a little grumpy? Yeah, you say, "What the heck? He thinks I'm an idiot."

Privately, I think you COULD be an idiot on any day at any moment. I don't really think you're an idiot all the time, but I do think we're all capable of being real stupid sometimes.

Make sure you paper trail it.

You will help yourself a lot and you've got to understand how sloppy we've become.

The third leading cause of death in America is medical error. "Researchers at John Hopkins University have calculated that mistakes from undetected complications to simple medication mix-ups account for more than 235,000 deaths a year."

The researchers later told the *Washington Post* it boils down to people dying from the care they receive rather than the disease for which they are seeking care.

The slop is everywhere. In most cases, it's trivial. But it's there and you must do whatever you can to make sure it doesn't slam the door shut on you or your business. It's not optional, it's mission critical.

Here's a sign from the bathroom at Robin Robins' office:

---

**BATHROOM ETIQUETTE**

Working in a small office with one restroom for everyone presents a few challenges. Please observe the following etiquette:

1. Always check the toilet seat. Make sure it is down AND CLEAN for the next person. Wipe any drips on the front of the toilet and floor. GUYS—this means you.

2. If toilet paper is running low, please get a

new roll out of the gray metal cabinet and put it on the toilet paper holder.

3. If you use the last of the paper towels, please alert Kathy to replace it.

4. If the wastebasket is full, either smash down the contents with your foot or go empty it.

5. Take a minute before leaving the restroom to make sure you left it in good shape for the next person. A courtesy shot of air freshener would be nice.

---

Note that this sign has been created for rational adults who are using an office bathroom. This is a big sign, not a tiny notice. It's on the wall.

And when I saw it, I said to myself "I've got to have it," because this is exactly how we need to go through life now. You have to assume everyone is an idiot, or, under the best of circumstances, they're not always idiots, but they could be idiots at any moment.

## THE LIMITS AND BENEFITS OF POSITIVE THINKING

Now let's talk about optimism and positive thinking within the context of accurate thinking.

There's a big difference between REASONED OPTIMISM and just optimism.

For many, there's confusion between optimism and entitlement—based on a misunderstanding of why and how money moves. Money does not move based on any sense of entitlement. If you believe you're entitled to rewards, they almost certainly will not come your way. Money runs from entitlement like an antelope from a prairie firestorm.

You CAN be optimistic about your own capabilities to create successful results. Optimistic about the overall condition of things or the future ... Possibly, optimistic about your own customers ... In the short term, optimistic about an investment or initiative ... All of the above tempered with recognition that *nothing and no one can be counted on, nothing is certain, guaranteed, or permanent.*

Being prepared for varied results is NOT a jinx.

Much unreasoned optimism, managerial negligence, and related disaster is born of ***superstition.*** (For example, the notion that even speaking the words "Murphy's Law" is being "negative" and setting in motion the mysterious attraction, even the inevitability, of encountering problems ... simply for uttering that phrase.)

Superstition is NOT accurate thinking ... but the power of "positive thinking" isn't 100 percent accurate either.

Dr. Norman Vincent Peale sold a lot of books stating the importance of positive thinking.

There's a difference between being a Pollyanna, expecting happy, positive results no matter what and having a pragmatic confidence in your ability to get a positive outcome.

The biggest misinterpretation of positive thinking is that it's the only thing required to achieving a positive outcome.

Napoleon Hill in *Think and Grow Rich* laid out his thirteen principles of success and one of the principles was **Accurate Thinking**.

It's the principle everybody likes the least. They love **Definiteness of Purpose** and they like **Enthusiasm**—but they don't like accurate thinking.

And that requires having an honest, truth-based appraisal of the world in which you function, of the people around you, of the opportunities around you, and of the problems inherent in your business.

It's like the salesperson desperately hoping nobody mentions objection number twelve and the flaw in his product, rather than fixing the flaw or bringing it up and figuring a way to sell around it.

Most people are not operating based on truth. It's very pragmatic to accept actual limitations, which is contrary to the militant positive thinking that anybody can do anything that they put their mind to … that's just not reality.

Renegade Millionaires operate from a premise of truth and reality. Accuracy not fantasy. That enables you to look at things as they really are instead of seeing what you wish. You see what is there and the opportunities that DO exist.

## From Hustling Lawnmowing Jobs to $6,000 a Day!

I'm just a young landscaping guy, thirty-five, and five years ago I was hustling jobs and learning horticulture, mowing lawns and shoveling driveways, looking for riches and looking for a thought leader with a model for tangible Main Street riches.

Now I own a $6,000-a-day in revenue tree service with 35 percent profit and always improving. That's $2,000 a day of profit! Financially, my life is what I hoped it could be. And most importantly, I ONLY work with people I choose, affluent people who appreciate me.

I set an example of efficiency and professionalism in my industry, I publish two newsletters with 2,000-person circulation and I'm a Kid Wonder among the other heavyweight landscape companies in my area. I have freedom to travel a lot and my voice has weight in the community.

And some days I sign a couple of dozen checks that come in the mail until my hand hurts, and when that happens, I think of you telling us to "never let anyone else sign the checks."

I am now committed as a Peak Performance/Renegade Millionaire Mastermind member and a big supporter of Adam going forward.

**Andrew Bachman**

# Eight-Figure Exit, Made Possible Because I Didn't Make a BIG Mistake

About one to one-and-a-half years ago, I was not happy with my business and the industry I was in. I was under regulatory pressures and not looking at a great future for my business as an energy supply company owner in NY.

I was looking at medical billing as an option. ***Dan told me that giving up all my experience in my industry may be a mistake.*** That statement hit home and made me think twice.

Then at SuperConference Dan said in his presentation that one way to grow your business was—***Take what you are doing successfully in one place and do it in another place.***

That's when I decided to do exactly what we were doing in NY and do it in New Jersey. That has been successful and the regulatory pressures in NY backed off.

As a result, we continued to make a seven-figure income and now my partner and I have an $18 million letter of intent to sell the business.

This is all from everything I have learned from you Dan. I have a fifteen-year-old boy with cerebral palsy. Now with the money from this sale and my savings, I can leave this earth knowing he will be taken care of for the rest of his life.

**Stephen Mellis**

*South Bay Energy*

# SECRET #6—CREATE A COMPETITION-FREE ZONE

One of the questions that almost always gets asked in a consultation setting goes like this:

> *"Tell me about your competition and who is your most formidable competitor?"*

If it's an auto repair business, they'll talk about the do-it-yourselfer and the neighborhood guy in the garage who works for next to nothing.

If it's a brick-and-mortar retailer, like a pet store or similar, they'll tell you all about Walmart and Amazon and perhaps some online version in their category, PetCrap.com or whatever.

Nowadays, given their market dominance, you'll hear a lot of people naming Amazon as their #1 challenge.

The orthodontist is going to define it as the dentist who does Invisalign for half the price he does, and the lawyer is going to define it as LegalZoom.com.

These are the types of answers you'll hear from business owners and their staff members when asking this kind of question.

It's a relatively small number of people who know, understand, and honestly believe that in reality, their most formidable competitor is THEM.

To a great extent, in many cases, all the rest is nearly irrelevant. If it wasn't, you would see more wholesale wipeouts of categories of business by the thing they consider most formidable.

Today it's Amazon, but in the days when Walmart was the new Godzilla on the block, there was an entire industry of us springing up as the up-against-the-Walmart guys, including the guy who wrote the book *Up Against Walmart*. There was an industry of speakers and consultants running around and feeding off the hysteria and panic that every time Walmart came to town it was going to kill everybody else in every kind of business.

That hysteria is still out there. There are cities and city councils that mobilize to block a Walmart store because it will kill off all the independent retailers as soon as it moves in.

The empirical evidence, however, is that this is at best a 50-50 proposition. So, some die and disappear when Walmart opens the doors. Others thrive as they have never thrived before. And other independents open as close to the new Walmart as they possibly can in order to feed off all the traffic—and they do well.

Your most formidable competitor remains YOU—whether Walmart or Amazon or anybody else waltzes into town.

For sure, Bezos at Amazon put a big dent in the independent bookstore industry. But survivors always prosper by the death of others. And when you look a little deeper, you'll see behavioral differences in the remaining bookstores that have nothing to do with what Amazon does or doesn't do—and definitely has nothing to do with price.

Instead they are running a very different business under the heading of a bookstore—in much the same way as Steve Adams' pet stores weren't pet stores, they were really pet service centers … with a nutritional counselor, and a trainer, and a dog washer, and "Oh, by the way, we sell the same stuff you can order from Amazon."

These bookstores are doing the same thing … author events, seminars, cooking classes, bus trips to the theater, and "Oh, by the way, we sell the same books you can order from Amazon."

So you can create your Competition-Free Zone—it just takes a willingness to "run toward the fire" rather than away from it. Here's a list of some effective strategies to make this happen:

### 1. Stand Out.

Number one is to figure out a way to stand apart from everybody else … preferably with something nobody else can or will duplicate, which usually is not found in or not sustainable in the product.

It's often by position more than it is product. It's being willing to say things and stand for things that everybody else is afraid of getting within ten feet of.

Take a stand. Drive a stake in the ground. Be willing to offend as well as attract.

Colin Kaepernick is a perfect example. Loathe him or love him, he's definitely driven a stake in the ground and set teeth on edge. The NFL can't run away fast enough. But Nike is more than happy to shovel boatloads of money in his direction.

Many businesspeople are reluctant to stand apart, not because of what works but because of a bunch of other political peer considerations. But it is by far the best no-competition strategy.

### 2. Raise Your Status

Next one is raise your status everywhere you can. Stand above everybody else.

For example, being an author and writing a book—well, seven or ten years ago that was a big part of this. Now it's just the ante to be at the table.

Get published by Advantage|ForbesBooks—well

that changes it again.

Write ten books, oh that changes it again.

Write a book with a famous coauthor ... that changes it again.

Write a book revealing the way you're doing it ... I'm going to tell my whole business story as a novel instead of ... that changes it again.

Being known as a speaker ... well yeah, twenty years ago that changed the game. Then it became the ante. Now, did you speak at Harvard? Did you get shot up in a space capsule and coach the astronauts while they flew around?

So, to achieve status, you look for a way to be above everybody else.

### 3. Show up Alone

Show up all alone in everything you do and every way you can. Find ways to put yourself and your prospects in a place where there's nobody else there when you are selling—it's only you and them.

It should be a simple principle to grasp.

If you are a fat, ugly, truly disgusting man, and

you want to pick up a woman, your odds are best if she has a broken-down car that she is standing next to in the middle of nowhere and there are wolves baying in the background from the woods. You stop; you're picking her up. End of story.

If you try and do it in a crowded bar where there are reasonably good-looking men available, you're probably sunk.

So, show up in a place that you control where you and they are alone together.

### 4. Strong Pre-Determination

Set it up so that it's practically a given that the prospect will do business with you right from the very beginning of your interactions and relationship. This is the purpose of the shock and awe package, it's the purpose of the survey they fill out, it's the purpose of getting a deposit before starting the job.

For example, there's a guy known for doing turnkey kitchen remodels, with brick ovens and everything that goes with them. Rather than offer a free consultation, he shifted his process to charging a fee beforehand:

*"$750 or I don't show up."*

That's unheard of in the industry, and furthermore, he's in the UK. So, it's not only unheard of in the UK, it's terribly impolite.

But as he's driving up to his consult's home, he knows immediately not only was he right to charge the deposit, but he probably charged too little. Because he's driving up to a mansion that if the people in Downton Abbey had money, this is where they would live.

He closes a $25,000 sale.

Without the deposit, the likelihood of closing the sale would've been less. The likelihood of closing it on the first call would've been less, and the elasticity to the final $25,000 deal would've been less or at least harder to get.

But with that $750 deposit to just show up, he helped create predetermination of, "Okay. We're going to hire this guy if we can."

The more hoops you can make prospects jump

through, the more sunken costs they have, the more time and other investment they have in buying from you, the more likely they are to buy and the more price elastic they are going to be about buying.

### 5. Exploit Time Invested

Exploit time invested because the time you spend alone with your prospect matters a great deal.

For example, with the SunSetter Awning people, if they have any brains, they have their in-home sales consultation choreographed so the salesperson is at the home for a long period of time before the prospect can get rid of him.

Because the longer he's there, the higher his odds of closing a sale because Ma and Pa have invested more time ... and that includes the time spent after going through the shock and awe package, making themselves some popcorn, sitting down to watch the DVD ...

And regarding that DVD, everybody says, "Oh, you should only make your sales pitch seven minutes long." No, no, no, no. Here's how long I want it to be. How much can we fit on a DVD? That's my question. I want it that long.

First of all, it isn't an online video sales letter where it's easy to close the window or go check Facebook or something. It's a much bigger hassle to stop once started—after all, they've got popcorn; they've got the dog in the lap; they found a DVD player; they found the right remote; they got the thing in the DVD player.

They're going to watch.

How many of you have driven to the theater, the movie stinks, and you still stayed halfway, three quarters, all the way to the end? If you were at home and got it on Netflix, how long would you have stayed? Five minutes! But in this situation you invested the time to go to the theater, so you watch the crappy movie longer.

Every time we raise time invested ... sales conversion increases. Miracle Ear's conversions were nearly doubled even with crappy salespeople. All they did was double the length of time of the exam. Didn't do anything else, just stretched the freaking exam.

Now, Ma and Pa are sitting there for an hour and a half instead of forty-five minutes. They're more likely to buy because they invested more time.

Same crappy salespeople, same god-awful presentation, same crappy close.

What else could they do? Put waiting time in between every one of these eight exams and stretch the time Harriet and Bob had to sit there. Bingo, up goes the conversion rate.

So, never underestimate the power of time invested by the prospect.

### 6. Work In a Sales-Conducive Environment

Here's a big one—always work in an environment that is conducive to selling.

Here's a typical chiropractor. Doesn't matter if it's 1979, or a typical chiropractor in 2020.

They go to all the trouble to get a prospective patient to come to the office for a diagnostic exam. They run ads in the local papers. They're on radio and they've got a Saturday morning talk show. They're doing everything known to man to get this person in for this exam.

They've spent money, they've spent time, they've spilled blood. Now they do the exam, take the x-rays, do all that, and now either then or when you come back, they are going to do the sales presentation, which they call a "report of findings."

Most of them do it in one of two locations in their office. Either in the treatment room, so you are sitting on a treatment table with no back. You have a bad back. By the way, this never occurs to them. Every time I point it out to them, it's like, "Huh?"

So, you have Bob and his wife sitting on the treatment table. Her feet don't reach the ground, they're both incredibly uncomfortable. You have a lightbox wedged over in the corner, so they are sitting there looking at the lightbox. They have neck pain. Every time I've explained this, this has surprised the doc.

They are sitting here doing this to look at the lightbox, which, by the way, now they can't see anyway because they're fifty and their vision sucks, but they're looking at the x-rays, and he's standing way over there now, because that's where the lightbox is, with his twisty spine.

Now when it comes time to show you the investment, how do I show you this? There's no table. There's no pad. There's no nothing.

This is selling scenario number one.

Selling environment number two is in his office, which is roughly the size of two phone booths. It has his lunch, his spare clothes, the dog, the dog bed, piles of paper, CDs he hasn't listened to, all this crap.

He leads Harry and Marge in, turns them sideways, takes something off of a chair, gets them down in the chair. This is his closing room and here's what nine out of ten say when you say, "You ought to have a closing room." "Oh, I don't have any space for that, and it would be too expensive. I don't want to spend the money to create a closing room."

Of course not. Let's spend all the money on advertising and marketing to bring people into an environment that is designed in the worst possible way to close a sale. Let's do that.

That makes all the sense in the world, but think

of how many people do it.

### 7. Use Overwhelming Force To Acquire Customers

Winning is rarely done gently. Really great coaches run up the score; they are not well liked. But the coaches everybody knows … the coaching legends of college football … Bear Bryant, Woody Hayes, Nick Saban …

*They ran up the score.*

They didn't just beat you; they left you so demoralized, you couldn't play the game for another three years. They wanted you weeping when you left the field to go to the locker room.

Bear kept the first string in most games, and they were up by fifty, "Kill them; we want them dead, laying on the ground."

It's the same thing in business.

Bezos isn't trying to just win; he's trying to dominate categories, he's trying to be a category killer.

When you commit to using overwhelming force in your business, it means the more you can spend on customer acquisition, the more successful, unassailable, and invulnerable you will be.

The secret of those who get rich by DOMINATION of a target market is they have structured the economics of their business to support "overwhelming force" spending—both to acquire customers and then to keep them.

The mistake made by most businesses is to try, in every way, to spend as little as possible to acquire customers. This severely restricts their ability to leverage multiple media options—at best they can use them sparingly—and it also limits their ability to nurture customers they have obtained.

The Renegade Millionaire does exactly the opposite … and is thus able to use ALL media options aggressively and can invest dynamically to nurture and keep customers acquired.

Let's say I ask a business owner: "What is the cost for you to get a customer?

"Well, $86."

"What do you think the average is in your industry?"

"I think I'm probably right about in the middle.

There are some people who spend a little more, I think that some people spend a little less."

My response would be this:

"Let's add a zero and then figure out how you can spend $860."

"I don't want to spend $860."

They do … and here's why:

> *"Because you will walk around and watch everybody else in your category, in your marketplace, in dire despair. You will see them just fold up and quit out of frustration. You will be reviled in your industry. So, of course, you want to spend $860, let's figure out how to do that."*

Normal entrepreneurs focus on how to reduce the cost per lead.

A Renegade Millionaire is always looking for ways to pay more for leads. This is so diametrically opposed to ordinary people's thinking that it does in fact qualify as a secret.

Actually, it's more than just a secret—it's a

strategic decision to constantly work to find a way to engineer the overall economics of their business that will allow them to spend virtually anything to get a lead and not care.

And the reason to do that is they can then advertise in places no one else can advertise. They can advertise MORE than anybody else can advertise. They can do more marketing than anybody can do ever. They can market practically without restriction and every option's open to them.

For example, Ben Altadonna is an information marketer to chiropractors. Ben has run full-page ads, sometimes two-page ads, in a trade journal every week. Competitors come and go constantly … in fact, there are five or eight or ten competitors all the time. But it's not the same ones because they're dying almost as soon as they start.

The big difference is he doesn't care what he spends to make a sale. He'll spend $1,000 or even more, $1,500 to get the customer. He can do this because he's got the rest of his economics engineered to make so much money on the customer, and so quickly once he has them, that he can afford to pay more than anyone else to get a customer.

This is the difference between sprinting and running a marathon—it gives you marathon power. It gives you staying power.

Imagine if you could get all the website traffic you wanted because nobody else can afford to spend more than you can spend.

This gives you an extraordinary competitive advantage—because you now own this media and that media and everybody else has to drop out because they can't stay. You own the entire marketplace and unless somebody jumps in again, you may even get to start spending less because you're the only one there.

That's the difference—everybody's over here trying to pinch pennies to reduce the cost of a lead. We're over here trying to figure out how we can spend more even on media that doesn't work that well, where the response returns are horrible and the cost per lead is ungodly, but it does deliver customers.

The whole issue here becomes your front-end transaction size for the first purchase … and then everything that happens after that.

Some businesses can do this because they have deep pockets and can handle going negative for a while. Others bridge that gap with continuity programs, where you whack their card every month. The best option for many is to immediately offer an upsell, and/or series of upsells, which increases the average value of that initial transaction.

This thinking is so foreign to the ordinary businessperson, to the ordinary small business person ... and it's even foreign to true entrepreneurs. I mean they don't, they can't get it and so they're restricted, horribly restricted by the initial transaction size and its profit.

What Renegade Millionaires do is liberate themselves from that restriction and make it go away.

### 8. Create Irresistible Offers

A lot of people build their marketing backwards.

They work on the sales letter, the promotional campaign, the website, the social media.

The last thing they deal with is the offer.

It's at the end of the sales letter, it's at the end of the ad, therefore they deal with it at the end.

But creating an Irresistible Offer should be #1 on the list.

People will suspend their skepticism, suspend their common sense, will move heaven and earth to get to that kind of offer.

And most people don't spend enough time creating the most powerful offers that they can right from the very beginning of the process.

If you watch Renegade Millionaires who are visible to everybody, and you watch how they sell in print or how they sell from the stage, or how they sell through their sales people on the phone or one-on-one, they tend to have fairly complicated multilayered offers with discounts and premiums and multiple guarantees.

It's not a plain vanilla, simple offer.

It's designed and crafted to be extremely powerful and extremely compelling.

## I Wasn't a Chiropractor, I Was a Marketer of Chiropractic Services

In 1997 everything changed for me.

It was the year that I purchased a marketing course co-created by Dan Kennedy. Prior to discovering Dan, I looked at the world and chiropractic like pretty much every other chiropractor.

Dan taught me to focus on the market, the customer, the patient.

I also learned ...

How to use media

How to write copy

How to test and track

How to generate and convert leads

How to run a business

How to think accurately ... and so much more

I learned from Dan that I wasn't a chiropractor but rather, I was a marketer of chiropractic services.

I learned that you can make way more money marketing what you do than you ever can doing what you do.

I learned how to value my time and what to do with that information.

I learned how to spend money to make money.

It would behoove you to consume everything Dan Kennedy that you can get your hands on.

**Dr. Ben Altadonna DC**
*ChiroTrust*

---

# SECRET #7—INVENT LESS, IMPLEMENT MORE

People really like "Creating" more than "Implementing."

There's an old "Hell" joke that illustrates this perfectly.

> A new batch of people arrives at the podium, the Devil's checking them in, and the first guy is a really big guy.
>
> The Devil says, "This is a bad place to be. You are going to be here forever. We try and let a person have one thing they like."

The big guy says, "I'm 600 pounds. I like to eat." The Devil says, "Okay, we'll make you the clean-up guy in a buffet, and you get all you can eat by working in a buffet."

Next guy up, he's got a shirt open to his waist. He's got gold chains around his neck, a car sales guy from Miami and the Devil says, "What's your deal?" The guy says, "I'm a sex addict. The idea of eternity without a lot of sex ..." The Devil says, "Okay, we'll make you the towel guy in the brothel and every third Friday you'll get all you want for free." The guy says, "Great."

Next guy, three-piece suit, tie, briefcase. The Devil says, "What's your story?"

He says, "I'm a salesman."

"What do you want?"

"Another brochure."

If you're a sales manager, you get it instantly.

Sales guys all want to go invent more sales aids. That's what they want to do. They are always coming and asking for more sales aids, "We need another brochure, we need another PowerPoint presentation. We need another Video Sales Letter."

If you have somebody doing social media marketing for you, they'll be in your office every day wanting you to do another video. "We need another video. We need another video. We need another video. We need another product. We need another product. We need another promotion. We need another this. We need another that."

That's NOT what you want.

*You want to find something that works and use it until it stops working.*

Not when you're bored with it, not when you're itching to try something new, not when your creative juices are flowing with a brand-spanking-new idea.

When it stops working. Otherwise keep using it.

There's an auto repair shop that mails to new homeowners. The piece looks like it comes from the kids. It's junky looking, done in crayon, and tells the prospect to come into dad and mum's auto store.

They've been mailing it to new movers every month for nine years. Still works.

That's what you want.

This is not what most people aspire to. In part, they're sucked into all this new stuff that does not even permit evergreen for the most part. It destroys evergreen. You wind up working for your media instead of your media working for you.

I want the crayon letter, and I want the crayon letter at the mail house, and every month the mail house gets the new mover list, and the crayon letter goes out. That's what I want.

If you've got stuff that works, figure out how to max that.

## IMPLEMENT MORE, INNOVATE LESS.

Most people do the opposite because the invention and the innovation feels good.

Trouble is, a lot of *the boring stuff is what makes*

*the money.*

For nine years, we had the Gold by the Inch TV show on the air. Client had a bad habit of watching his own show. The shows don't change, you understand. It's a half hour infomercial.

He was literally leaving the TV on every night when he went to bed because he wants to wake up and see his show. His wife moves out of the bedroom because it's insane.

He's watching his show three hundred times a month. It isn't that good. Shot the whole thing for $18,000.

One day he says to me: "Everybody has seen it. We've got to do a new show."

"No, you've seen it enough for everybody. Everybody hasn't seen it. You're carrying the whole load of viewership here on your own shoulders. Go to sleep."

"By now, everybody has seen it."

"Show me the numbers. Is there any decline?"

"No."

"So please, go do something boring that will

make you more money. Leave this alone, go focus on the media buying. See if you can squeeze another 10 percent out of the media buying. Go add another step to the back-end sequence to the unconverted leads. Mystery shop your phone telemarketers every day instead of every three days. Do some boring stuff that maximizes the thing we have, that works like a charm and leave it alone. Run it more but leave it alone."

Everybody does this.

They're screwing around with the thing that should be left alone and not doing all the boring crap to squeeze the last ounce of juice from it. *That's what you want to do.*

And one of the most important, boring things you should make sure happens is this …

## CREATE PROCESSES, NOT JUST PRODUCTS

Many great businesses are thought of as product businesses by their customers, by the public, even by their investors, when in reality, they are process businesses.

The real key to their ability to thrive is all about their process, and how good they are once they get a lead or a prospect or a customer.

Almost all retail businesses have terrible processes in place. In fact, most retailers actually don't have a process. This is making it easier for Amazon to kill them than it would be otherwise.

- They have stuff on the shelves.
- They have a cash register.
- They manage to get the lights turned on in the morning.
- They have somebody there to take the money.
- They hope somebody comes in.

This is it.

Their process with a customer is hope they put the right stuff in the bag, hope the clerk didn't say something to you that thoroughly pissed you off, and hope you'll come back and buy more of it when you need it.

I just described the whole process.

Most restaurants, what is their process?

- You show up.
- They feed you.
- You pay.
- You leave.
- They hope you come back.

I just described the whole process.

Bezos is looking at this; he's saying, "We've got process over here. We know."

See, most retailers don't even have the most basic process.

Here's a strategy Hickory Farms in 1983 paid a big chunk of change for—probably close to a quarter million dollars.

Make a little chart for the person at the cash register.

If they buy cheese and not sausage, look at the chart and say this:

- *"You know, what most people like with that cheese is this kind of sausage. Would you like to have some sausage, too?"*

If they buy sausage and not cheese, she looks on the chart, and she says …

- *"You know, what most people like with that sausage is this kind of cheese. Would you like to have some cheese, too?"*

This is what they got for all that money. This isn't new. You can find examples of this from the forties at least.

But, how many places do you go at the retail level where there is some equivalent of that dynamic, where you are buying something and somebody could easily suggest, "You know, because you're buying that, you might also need, want, be able to use, benefit from, like this. Would you like me to fetch it for you?" It never happens.

Nobody asks except at Christmas, sometimes at Father's Day … you could go out, and eat out in a good restaurant every night of the year, pay your bill, and never get asked if you'd like gift cards. Never. How brain-dead stupid is this?

You won't be asked for your contact information, and you won't be asked for your birthdates. See, they have no process.

The retail store has no process. The best they've got is, "Let us sign you up for our little club." If they're part of a national chain, they've usually got that. If you go to a Hallmark store, there's a Hallmark Gold Club, and "We can sign you up, and you'll get discounts," but they have no real process.

Amazon has a process, including the sausage and cheese process. You don't get to buy a book without being told, "Hey, if you like that book, and that guy, you would probably like these books." They've got a process.

Their brick-and-mortar counterparts have no process, or barely a process.

So, process is really important. It's how you turn an okay business into a really profitable business.

Amazon is dangerous because these guys understand process. Most of those whom they are killing don't understand it, and if they understand it, they're not willing to take precautionary action.

The principle is this:

**It isn't just what happens.**
**It's how it happens.**
**It's where it happens.**
**It's when it happens.**

The better the process, the more the money.

Another last boring, but critical task you can do instead of inventing …

## DO WHAT EVERYONE ELSE WON'T DO—BUILD A BOND

Let's say you're in a business that should be a commodity—menswear.

There's plenty of competition. You might think that your number one task would be to constantly come out with new jackets, new pants, new shoes, new new new.

But you don't have to. Because it's not that difficult really to prosper against the chains.

Independently owned retailers can do things that the chains cannot do … and first and foremost that involves really communicating with your customers.

> *"They're getting mailing pieces from us. They're getting a voice broadcast six times a year. They're getting personal phone calls from their sales associates four to five times a year. They're getting emails from us every week."*

And truthfully, these are things the big chains just don't do, don't understand, and don't value.

But independent retailers can do all this and more—and build a much stronger bond with their customers and clients. People like dealing with a place that cares about them.

## My Next Business I Want to Run from a Laptop in Lake Tahoe!

Through Dan Kennedy I learned that I could take charge of my future and build the kind of life I wanted. I remember you saying, "The big trick in America is not making a lot of money. ***The big trick is doing it in a way that is personally fulfilling and provides a lifestyle you love."***

That stuck with me as I began the long, difficult journey of digging myself out of a life I profoundly disliked. In 2002 I wrote in my journal, "My next business I want to run from a laptop in Lake Tahoe." I didn't know exactly what that meant, but I had a vision of the kind of life I wanted: plenty of money and freedom to move and travel at will and live where I wanted.

In 2007 that vision finally became a reality when I began Flooring Success Systems, an information marketing and group coaching business for flooring retailers. Since then we've added marketing services and private coaching.

I've written three books for flooring retailers, I'm a columnist for a major industry trade magazine, and I speak at industry events. In other words, I've implemented many of the positioning strategies you teach. As well as countless other strategies I learned from you.

Currently, my wife and I run our business from Colorado. We plan to be here for a few months, maybe until next Spring. We'll see. We spent last year living in various places in California—including Lake Tahoe—spending time with family and friends.

While there I began a music recording project with two close friends. I fly fish regularly. Next week I start my first classes toward earning my skydiving license. We spent several months living in the Virgin Islands, as well as Florida and other places, all while running our business remotely.

As I read back over this it sounds like one of those cheesy "live the life of your dreams" ads, but it's all true. And here's the funny thing: **this has been my "normal" for over a decade**. And so much of it is due to your help.

Dan, without your teachings and strategies, including giving me "permission" to build my business around my life, I simply wouldn't be here. More than once I've thanked God that I found you.

Thank you for all that you have done to impact my life, and the lives of thousands of other entrepreneurs. It's been a long, long time since I felt the profound darkness and hopelessness of my early thirties, and I owe so much of that to the direction you provided.

**Jim Armstrong**
*Flooring Success Systems*

# READY TO SPIT IN THE EYE OF THE WITCH?

Years ago at a mastermind meeting, Dr. Jim Fairfield talked about running a very aggressive promotion for his practice at a time of year regarded as "slow" by his entire profession.

He called it "spitting in the eye of the village witch."

*Renegade Millionaires LOVE to Spit in the Eye of the Witch.*

- Industry norms are to be violated.
- Rules are for mere mortals.
- The 212 ways it can't be done are irrelevant as

soon as you find one way it can.

- Criticism from others, be immune to it.

Most people FEAR the village witch. They do everything they can not to draw her attention, not to provoke her.

Actually, most people go through life like the painfully shy kid in the classroom or frightened pedestrian on a dark street at night; they actually shrink themselves and pray they go unnoticed.

Your industry peers will tell you, "Go along with the crowd. Don't make waves."

When Bill McGowan at MCI challenged the entire telephone industry and the federal government and said, "Who says AT&T owns long-distance?" he spit in the eye of the village witch.

Similarly, when O'Steen took the prohibition on lawyers advertising, when the chiropractic profession sued the American Medical Association, they spit in the eye of the village witch.

When Disney ignored all expert advice and built the first amusement park with a single entrance/exit, he spit in the eye of the village witch.

After the fact, of course, everybody celebrates such courageous folks who win. Those who lose may be cursed, reviled, imprisoned, boiled in oil. There is danger.

I don't think you need to go looking for trouble. But I don't think you can prosper living fearfully or timidly either. Healthy, prudent paranoia, yes. Fear or timidity, no.

Want to know a secret about witches?

**The secret is** … they have no power unless you give it to them.

**Most of the "boogeymen" that bedevil us in our businesses … in our lives … are powerless except for the power we hand them.** We agree to be governed by them. We drop to our knees on our own.

**Consider the "indispensable" employee holding employer, co-workers, office hostage.** Time and time and time again, I hear of the existence of such a mythical, powerful creature from Magnetic Marketing coaching group members and clients. Time and time again, after extended periods of suffering, when finally emboldened to slay this demon, or the demon abruptly exits on its own, the myth is exposed.

The employee was far from indispensable. In fact, the removal of the creature instantly improved every measurable aspect of the business. It could have been sooner rather than later if only the entrepreneur had seen the creature for what it really was.

Or consider the troublesome, unreasonable, impossible-to-satisfy client holding the vendor hostage … the "rules" of an industry, the way things "must" be done, the prices that "can't" be raised, the business that is "different."

Look more courageously at whatever fire-breathing, seemingly all-powerful creature stands between you and the way you want things to be. Its power exists only so long as you acknowledge it as powerful.

If you want to become a Renegade Millionaire you need to take this lesson to heart.

If there are creatures out there holding you back, bedeviling you, that you are infusing with power …

spit in the eye of the thing bullying you. It'll shrink instantly. Cower and slink away.

The only opinion that ever matters is the opinion backed up by money changing hands.

Therefore, the customer who gives you money counts a lot.

---

### "THEY'RE THE ONES WHO PAY THE BILLS"

Mark Cuban, owner of the NBA's Dallas Mavericks basketball team and *Shark Tank* member, was once interviewed and all the trouble he got into with the NBA was brought up. He set a record for fines as an owner. They asked him about having a reputation for not caring what others think. And he said this: *"No. We don't care what other people think. I don't even care what I think. The only thing I care about is what the fans think. Because they're the ones who pay all the bills."*

---

## THE PURPOSE OF A RENEGADE MILLIONAIRE BUSINESS

Renegade Millionaires understand the purpose of having a business. They live by a very basic personal finance principle as noted in the book *The Richest Man in Babylon.*

### Pay Yourself First

Here's how it typically works. You pay everybody else, you pay all the bills, if there's anything left, you take some, right? Problem is, quite often there's nothing left.

So you go take some that you took before and put it back in, right? Don't you think? Most entrepreneurs? Sure. And it's exactly wrong. It's the polar opposite of how the game needs to be played.

Here's how the game needs to be played. *You get paid first,* and if you can't get paid, then the whole deal's bad and you should get out of it as quickly as you possibly can.

As a Renegade Millionaire, your job is to extract

wealth from your business on a day-to-day, week-to-week, month-to-month, year-to-year basis, and accumulate your wealth outside of your business.

Basically, most people have erroneous ideas about the very purpose of business.

- Liberals would have you believe that the purpose of business is to employ people.
- Government thinks the purpose of business is to pay taxes, right? That's what they think the purpose of business is.
- Communities think the purpose of business is to provide for the general welfare.
- And too many businesspeople think the purpose of business is to free them from having to work for a boss.

Renegade Millionaires understand that your business is a tool, a device, a means of creating money to build wealth.

It's a different paradigm and very few people make that paradigm shift.

## THE INSANE PLEASURES OF BEING A RENEGADE MILLIONAIRE

- **Being profoundly superior to the morons and mere mortals surrounding you.** Yes, it is immensely satisfying to know so much that they do not know. To watch the highly educated MBAs and lawyers on shows like *The Apprentice* who couldn't run a lemonade stand in the real world. To look at big, dumb corporations and revel in their self-destruction.

- **Firing a client or a customer.** As hard as they are to get, you might think there'd be no pleasure in this. And usually, there isn't. But *being able to,* there's enormous pleasure in *that.*

- **Taking a Wednesday or a week off.** Or enjoying coffee on your backyard deck while all of your neighbors are climbing into cars and crawling into a bumper to bumper commute. Or having neighbors wonder about you—*what is he anyway?*

- **Alchemy**. Making money materialize out of thin air. Conceiving some offer or promotion or ad or mailing, bringing it to life, and watching money pour in. I wonder, what is more satisfying than *that*? I know for a fact that Gene Simmons gets more satisfaction from filling the arena, the ticket sales, the merchandise sales, than he does from performing, just as I did from speaking. Anybody can play rock music. When you see customers streaming into your store, your event, buying your book or gadget or bottle of glop on a store shelf, your commercial on TV, your ad in a magazine—you've got to *FEEL* something special, because you're doing something comparatively few have the guts to do. Most everybody *wants* to. Few do. Most haven't got the guts.
- **Resiliency**. Oddly, successful Renegade Millionaires relish their war stories of disaster

and recovery even more than their outright successes. Maybe not so oddly. Unlike anyone else, the entrepreneur is totally in control of his own redemption. There's pleasure in that.

- **Wealth**. Well, of course. To quote, I've been poor, I've been rich, rich is better. It isn't perfect. You don't have $500 problems anymore; you have $50,000 and $500,000 problems. Still. It's better.

## THE RENEGADE MILLIONAIRE'S MOST IMPORTANT LESSON

I was once asked, "What's the most important lesson you've ever learned and behavior you've adopted related to your business and financial success?"

My answer:

> *"The idea of putting yourself into a position where you own and control the single most important and expandable asset there is, which is a loyal cadre of a sufficient number*

*of customers, clients, patients, whatever, who will consistently give you money. Then, if you have any kind of bill or financial need, all you need to do is think up or find another promotion, another product, another event and they'll give you what you need."*

# Four Things Dan Taught Me About Being a Renegade Millionaire

After a friend gave me his *No B.S. Direct Marketing* book, it didn't take me long to become a super fan of its author, Dan Kennedy. I became a member of his coaching group, ordered his top courses, and attended his events.

Here are the four lessons I learned from him that can change your business too

1. **There will always be a call to action**—Prior to being introduced to the teachings of Dan, I was the awareness campaign queen. I ran a public relations agency and was really good at "getting the names out there" of my clients and our firm. Dan introduced me to the concept of always including what you want the person to do next, without guesswork. From putting a call to action to opt-in to your webinar in a Facebook ad, to asking someone to sign up for notifications on your website at the end of your blog and asking for the sale at the end of a Facebook Live video.

   **There will always be a call to action. Because it works.**

2. **Marketing spend should be based on measured results**—Dan, however, introduced me to a way of marketing that is based on results. While you are getting results, spend more money. No results, don't spend any money.

3. **Whoever can spend the most to get a customer wins**—Instead of going after the cheapest possible leads, being able to spend the most for each of your campaigns will bring you to the finish line.

4. **One is the loneliest number**—Never rely on one source of traffic. Never ever, never.

   Facebook can kick you off tomorrow, your website can get hacked, Instagram may shut down … Always have more than one channel running at a time.

# THE RENEGADE MILLIONAIRE MANIFESTO

**Renegade Millionaire:** Is about transforming ordinary businesses into extraordinary wealth-producing assets. Its core ideas include:

- **The money pyramid**
    - 1 percent rich
    - 4 percent prosperous
    - 15 percent a good living
    - 60 percent struggle financially endlessly
    - 20 percent broke

- **There are five sources of power of a business**
  - Lists/relationship
  - Reputation—what you are known for
  - Marketing
  - Specific marketing advantage
  - Clarity
- **Accurate thinking.** People are who they are—not what you might prefer them to be. You need to be very, very careful whom you let in and weed out the bottom—employees, clients, vendors.
  - Coach the coachable; fire the rest. Fire fast and hire slow. Create exceptional opportunity for exceptional people. Manage profits not just people and reject all norms.
  - Opinions do not matter—facts matter, test results matter, and money matters.
  - You get what you pay for.

- **Organized effort.** Most people's efforts are not organized around any strict governance, organizing theory of business, philosophy or ethic, definite plan. Most effort is unmoored, reactive, and random. People and businesses easily lose their way.

  Renegade Millionaires are consistent; others are inconsistent. It is important to develop a system for organized effort that stays consistent with a set of guiding principles. This is what says yes or no to the constant stream of questions, strategic decisions, programs, solutions, opportunities, everything that the entrepreneur has to manage. MOST PEOPLE are using tactics in search of strategy.

**"Strategies without principles tend to dissolve in time or collapse under pressure"**
**—Dan Kennedy**

- **The Big Idea**. The best businesses are about

something (in addition to making money) at least in the minds of their patrons.

- **Reject ALL limitations and limiting definitions**. Both of others or your own. You can't see anything greater than the hole through which you're looking. Renegade Millionaires obtain information and ideas in greater quantity—both horizontally and vertically. They read, watch, listen, go, and buy. The world is your oyster—there are no boundaries, no limits, no lines to color inside of.
- **Time is the most perishable, irreplaceable asset** and must be treated as such in every way possible. You can't afford to start from scratch—Renegade Millionaires are not infatuated with creativity and invention (opportunity may be invented but the methods of its invention were not—they were just concealed) but instead infatuated with results, profit, and speed.
- **Commitment to what works**—regardless of

its age or youth. Old and new can co-exist; are not mutually exclusive. Beware of confinement by old, beware of seduction by new to abandonment of old.

- **Build it to last.** The long game, not the short game—present bank vs. future bank and simultaneous deposits. Most get customers to make sales, we make sales to get customers. You must have a true understanding of where the business's money actually comes from and where the *real* equity lies.
- **Operate in a competition-free zone of your making.** The first and chief objective of your advertising and marketing is to place the prospect into a competition-free zone where he gives you a considerable amount of his undivided attention, having come into the zone with a high level of predetermination to buy from you and only you.
- **Renegade Millionaires don't sell "stuff."** The crucial thing to remember is that we are

NOT selling a product at all, but are seeking to produce a psychological response. All the money is in the meaning—people buy for psycho-emotional reasons.

- **The timid, humble, and gentle must wait to inherit the earth.** There is no room for timidity in advertising, marketing, or selling.
- **The most valuable businesses are process businesses—not product businesses.** The more processes there are, the more complex and sophisticated, the more rigid (thus consistent), and the more enforced they are—the more money to be made.
- **The more you can/will spend on customer acquisition, the more successful, unassailable, and invulnerable you will be.** The majority try in every way to spend as little as possible, thus severely restricting themselves to few media options, used sparingly; and to severely limited "nurture" of customers once obtained. Renegade Millionaires do the

opposite—using all media options aggressively and able to invest dynamically in "nurture."

- **Invent less—implement more.** Carefully determine what the problem is and then focus on the REAL problem. Avoid the unending "re-decorating of room." Do the boring stuff, lock it, load it, and sell it.

## Instantly Access A Complimentary Renegade Millionaire Presentation By The Professor Of Harsh Reality, And THE Millionaire Maker Dan Kennedy Valued at $297.00!

This is a classic Dan Kennedy, NO HOLDS barred, unvarnished ninety-minute presentation from a live training where attendees each paid $4,997.00 to attend. We're giving you instant access to the presentation as our gift for investing in the Renegade Millionaire Book. Enjoy!

**Dan Kennedy Reveals**
**The Renegade Millionaire Secret Code ...**

- Find out why Disney CEO Bob Iger was gleeful when park attendance dropped by 10%! ***True Renegade Thinking!***
- Where do you fit in the 1%, 4%, 15%, 60%, 20% pyramid—and why this matters A LOT. Discover how *Renegade Millionaires apply this pyramid to business and life decisions in an instant.*
- **One Way To GUARANTEE you'll be perpetually frustrated and broke ...** Scary how many live this way.
- If you have just ONE of __________ **...** It's ***100% certain bad things will happen to you and your company***
- Discover one or two words _______________ that Renegade Millionaires ***use to drive every single decision they make.***

## ARE YOU READY TO BECOME THE NEXT RENEGADE MILLIONAIRE?

Take the 6 Question Renegade Millionaire Assessment
To Discover Your Renegade Millionaire Readiness Score at

**WWW.RENEGADEMILLIONAIRE.COM/BOOK**

## We'd Love To Have You Join Us At Our Next Renegade Millionaire Mastermind Event

**Get Your Renegade Millionaire Readiness Score and We'll See If You're Ready To Join Our Tribe Of Renegade Millionaire Entrepreneurs**

**WWW.RENEGADEMILLIONAIRE.COM/BOOK**